THE GREAT IRISH SCIENCE BOOK

PROFESSOR
LUKE O'NEILL

ILLUSTRATED BY
LINDA FÄHRLIN

GILL BOOKS

MEET YOUR GUIDES

THE GREAT IRISH SCIENCE BOOK
PROFESSOR LUKE O'NEILL

THE AUTHOR

Professor Luke O'Neill is from Bray, County Wicklow. He went to Presentation College, Bray, where his love of biology began (thanks, Mr Mooney!). He studied Biochemistry in Trinity College Dublin and then did a PhD in Pharmacology (the science of medicines) in London. He moved to Cambridge to work on immunology before returning to Trinity where he set up his own team of scientists to further explore the wonders of our immune system (see page 48). He hopes that his research might lead to new treatments for inflammatory diseases. He loves all of science – except the hard bits!

THE ILLUSTRATOR

Linda Fährlin is originally from Stockholm, where she studied art and design. After working in Australia for many years, she now lives with her family in Sligo, where she works from her studio near the Atlantic Ocean. On the drawing table, you'll find everything from schoolbooks and children's books to commercial commissions. Linda often draws inspiration from science and believes that art and science can both change the way we see the world. One of her favourite snippets of science is that colours can be mathematically explained as waves (see page 77). This could explain why Linda is drawn to the blue waves in the sea! When not illustrating or bobbing in the soothing ocean, Linda is studying how to maximise children's learning with the help of illustration.

CONTENTS

WELCOME ON BOARD! 02

THE UNIVERSE 04
The Big Bang 06
Inside the cosmos 08
Stars and galaxies 10
Our solar system 12
The Earth and moon 14
The Universe: The future 16
Be a scientist! 17

PLANET EARTH 18
Geology 20
Life and evolution 22
Dinosaurs 24
Animals 26
Human evolution 28
Plants 30
Habitats 32
Climate change 34
Planet Earth: The future 36
Be a scientist! 37

THE HUMAN BODY 38
The skeleton 40
The brain 42
The digestive system 44
The circulatory system 46
The immune system 48
The reproductive system 50
Cells 52
Genes 54
Life's building blocks 56
The microscopic world 58
The human body: The future 60
Be a scientist! 61

THE VERY SMALL 62
Matter 64
Atoms 66
Elements 68
Electricity 70
Magnetism 72
Force and motion 74
Waves 76
Energy 78
Light 80
Fundamental forces 82
The very small: The future 84
Be a scientist! 85

BON VOYAGE! 86
TIMELINE OF DISCOVERY 88
INDEX 90
THANKS 93

WELCOME ON BOARD!

Don't go too far or you will fall off the edge of the world.

How would you like to come on a journey with me? Watch out – it could be a trip that will change your life! But I can promise you lots of fun along the way.

I AM A SCIENTIST. I became a scientist because when I was younger, I was fascinated by how the world works. When I was told that the Wicklow Mountains had been carved out by massive glaciers 20,000 years ago, I thought 'NO WAY!' And I wanted to know more.

We all have moments like that, because humans are the nosiest of creatures. You might be sitting in a park on a nice summer's day. You've just had an ice-cream and you feel good! You look around you, and maybe you begin to wonder ...

... how FAR AWAY is the sun and why is it so HOT?

... why is the grass GREEN and how does it GROW?

... why can those birds FLY but I can't?

... how is my BODY using the ice-cream I just ate?

... beep – there goes my SMARTPHONE. How does that work?

Well, wondering about all these things makes you a scientist!

The thing about science is that it has been around since people were able to look at the world and wonder: why?

Think back: 100,000 years ago, your ancestors might have been sitting outside their cave, wondering why there was a bright fire in the sky. They might have wondered how to get at those tasty birds in the tree (because as far as we know, there was no ice-cream). They might not have had beeping smartphones, but wondering these things made them scientists too!

Humans have always ASKED QUESTIONS and tried to come up with ANSWERS. Sometimes the answers are right, and sometimes they need a bit of work. Down through the centuries, people have believed all sorts of things to be true. Things like ...

... the Earth is FLAT

... toothaches are caused by WORMS

... your personality is based on the LUMPS on your head

... MAGGOTS can grow from meat

... humans appeared on the Earth 6,000 YEARS AGO

But by using science, we have proved that these beliefs are WRONG! (Although some stubborn people are still hanging on to a few of them.) Science will keep proving things wrong every single day, and – hopefully – we'll keep getting closer to the TRUTH.

So, how does this amazing thing called science actually work?

It's all about coming up with an IDEA to explain something we see in the world around us. But that's not enough.

Next, we have to do an EXPERIMENT to test our idea. Experiments are very important to science as they give us information to support the idea.

Then, using this information, we come up with a THEORY that explains what we saw in the first place.

Let's think of an idea: Some things are good at catching fire, like wood. Maybe wood has a special ingredient that makes it burn well?

Idea:
Ice-cream made from fresh berries is really tasty!

Experiment:
Let's make ice-cream with fresh berries!

Tried and tested! It's great to be a scientist!

Theory:
The fresh berries give the frozen cream a rich flavour!

Better ask my friends to be sure!

The Right Answer:
Investigate more.

Hmm ... Can I please have another one? Just to make sure?

Well, next we need to test this. We weigh a stick of wood, then set it on fire. Don't burn your eyebrows! Now we weigh the burnt ashes, and we see that the ashes are lighter than the stick of wood.

So something has been lost when the wood burned. Ah-ha! There must be a special ingredient in wood that makes it flammable! Problem solved.

... But that's an easy answer. And science is not about easy answers – it's about RIGHT ANSWERS. So we can't stop there. We have to do our experiment again to make sure the same thing always happens. We need to test it in different ways, and from different perspectives, to make sure that it's not wrong.

If we do more experiments, we'll discover that the missing mass in the wood has actually been changed into a gas. There's no magical ingredient* – just a chemical reaction.

* Scientists actually did believe in this magic ingredient for a while – they called it phlogiston!

This tells us something important about how science works. Just because we think our idea is right doesn't mean it is. People can get things wrong, but scientists working together can look at NEW EVIDENCE, correct theories, and move closer to the truth. The person who came up with the first idea just has to accept that they were wrong (hopefully they didn't burn their eyebrows off for nothing).

A wise scientist once said: SCIENCE IS MORE THAN KNOWLEDGE. IT'S A WAY OF THINKING.

And that's what makes it so great.

So now that you've begun to **think** like a scientist, let's get started.

In this book, we'll go on an incredible scientific journey from the very, very BIG to the very, very SMALL. Starting with the universe itself, I will bring you through the galaxies and stars, down to our very own planet Earth and across its fabulous features, into our wonderful bodies and all their cells, and on down to the very elements and atoms that make up all things.

I will also tell you about how our little island of IRELAND has made huge contributions to science. And, even better, at the end of each section, I've given you a few EXPERIMENTS to try so you can be a scientist yourself.

Science is a small word for a really, really big thing. For everything in this book, there's a branch of science that studies it (yes, even poop). The great thing about science is how all these different areas work together. You might find you need to flick back and forward in this book to understand something, and that's all the better.

But for now, fasten your seatbelt, as I take you on this greatest journey of them all. But a word of warning ... YOU WON'T BE THE SAME AFTERWARDS!

THE UNIVERSE

Let's get started. A great place to begin is way out here in the universe. (Actually, it's the only place we *can* start – before the universe, we don't know what there was – if anything!)

People used to think that the sun went around the Earth and the stars were flaming torches in the sky. Over the centuries, scientists proved that the Earth goes around the sun, and that the stars are incredibly hot balls of fire billions of kilometres away. If you think that's hard to believe now, imagine trying to understand it 500 years ago ...

It's pretty amazing that humans have found out so much about our little planet and where it fits in the universe. We managed to invent telescopes to see far into space, and we've sent rockets, spaceships, satellites and even humans themselves up there too – just to see what's going on.

Now it's your turn. Strap yourself in for the most spectacular journey of your life: across billions and billions of kilometres and billions and billions of years back in time. Get ready to have your mind blown wide open by the majesty of the cosmos.

THE BIG BANG

You are very small. You're very special, of course, but you are a tiny, puny thing – at least compared to the **universe,** which is very big indeed. The universe is everything there is: all matter, time and space combined into one big thing.

And I mean big. Get ready, because we are about to deal with some very large numbers.

A BANGING BEGINNING

13.8 billion years ago …

(How can we possibly understand 13.8 billion years ago? Do you remember what happened last week? Or one year ago? Imagine when your grandparents were children. But a million years? 13.8 billion years? It seems crazy, but it's true.)

… the entire universe was squished inside a tiny bubble, thousands of times smaller than the head of a pin, and smaller again. There was nothing outside this single point, and no time for it to happen in! Then the bubble popped – the BIG BANG – and the universe was born. Time, space and matter all began in an instant, and all the building blocks of the universe began to spread outwards, until it reached the size it is today – which is ginormous!

It's so big that scientists aren't exactly sure how big it is, or even how to measure it. It's a bit like seeing the tusk, tail and toenail of an elephant, and then trying to figure out how big the elephant is! But we can use clever science and something called light years to give it a try.

POP

WHAT'S A LIGHT YEAR?

Well, it's not a year that went on a diet! Light travels at the incredibly fast speed of 300,000 kilometres per second. I bet that would make your head spin! (*See the light on page 80.*) One LIGHT YEAR is the distance that light travels in one year – 9.46 trillion kilometres.

Imagine you're in a race with light. The starting gun goes off and when you've taken one step, light will be 300,000 km ahead of you. Light will have gone around the world seven times. A cheetah would be left in its dust. Usain Bolt, the world's fastest runner, has no chance against light. It would take a tortoise over four years to go around the Earth just once!

Have you ever noticed that the light from a candle is fainter the further away you are from it? Well, in the same way, astronomers use the brightness of stars to measure distance. By measuring the time it takes their light to reach us, we can figure out how many light years away they are.

The nearest star to us (after the sun) is called Proxima Centauri, and it is 4.24 light years away. If you tried to drive there from your back garden, at 50 km/hr, it would take you around 90 million years to get there!

See you in 90 million years!

HEAVY

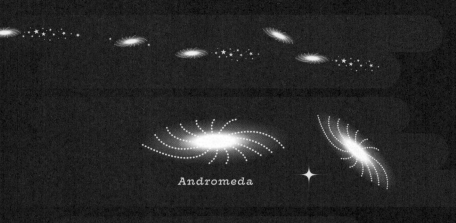

Andromeda

Proxima Centauri

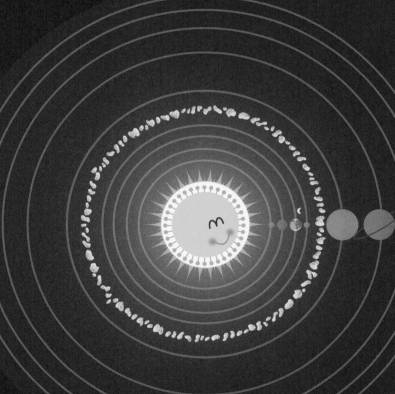

Galaxies
Far, Far Away

Nearby
Galaxies

The Stars

Our Solar System

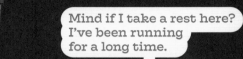

Mind if I take a rest here? I've been running for a long time.

IT ALL ADDS UP

Using this ladder, we can finally figure out the width of the universe, giving us ... drum roll ... **93 BILLION LIGHT YEARS**. A very, very big number indeed – perhaps the biggest number of them all. The word ginormous doesn't cover it.

IRISH CONNECTION

WILLIAM PARSONS

William Parsons, 3rd Earl of Rosse was an Anglo-Irish astronomer. During the 1840s, he had a huge telescope built at Birr Castle, County Offaly. Using this telescope, Rosse saw and recorded a large number of galaxies.

LADDER TO THE STARS

To measure the vast, vast distances in space, astronomers use a **COSMIC DISTANCE LADDER** – the most impressive ladder of all time.

- The first rung gets us to our solar system.
- The next gets us to the stars.
- The next gets us to galaxies that are nearby.
- The final rung gets us to galaxies far, far away.

INSIDE THE COSMOS

The universe is enormously huge. What could possibly fill all that space? Well, all that space!

Imagine the universe is a football. Let's look inside.

Only 5% of the universe is the stuff we can see – all the stars, planets and chunks of rock like asteroids, meteorites and comets.

Imagine a football...

With these things inside it:

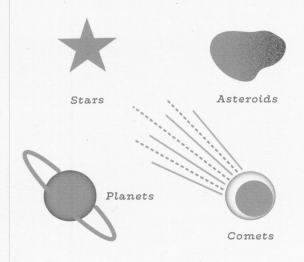

Stars

Asteroids

Planets

Comets

AN ATTRACTIVE IDEA

These stars and planets were all formed by a force of attraction called GRAVITY, which pulls together all matter (*gravitate to page 82 for more*). The more stuff, or MASS, something has, the greater the force of its gravity. That means really big objects like planets and stars have a strong gravitational pull.

The Earth's gravity is what stops us floating off into space. The sun has even stronger gravity, but we're far enough away that it doesn't pull us in ... phew!

FINDING THE ELEPHANT

A quarter of the rest of the universe is made of something called **DARK MATTER**. It's called this because we can't see or detect it, but astronomers are confident it must be there.

What? How can they know something is there without any proof?

Well, it's about looking at clues. Think about that elephant again. You can't see it, but you can touch its trunk, legs and back. You can guess it must be an elephant. Scientists use evidence like this to put together theories. They have figured out that without dark matter, all the galaxies in the universe would fly off in all directions, and may not even form at all. Dark matter is the anchor that holds everything together.

Some of the evidence for this is that galaxies aren't sprinkled evenly all over the universe. They occur in **CLUSTERS**, making up what's known as the **COSMIC WEB**. Dark matter holds these clusters together, a bit like water on a spider's web – each galaxy is a droplet and the web is dark matter. (Hopefully scientists won't find a giant spider ...)

Astronomers have seen other evidence in a spectacular cosmic event: two huge galaxy clusters colliding. At the outer edges of the collision, scientists could see light being bent by dark matter. Imagine, if there was noise in space (*there isn't - see why on page 77*) the sound of galaxies crashing into one another!

We're no WIMPs, we hold the universe together!

Scientists have a name for what they think dark matter is made of: Weakly Interacting Massive Particles, or WIMPs for short. But WIMPs are far from wimpy – they are the glue that holds everything in the universe together!

Scientists are trying to make **WIMPS** in a machine called the Large Hadron Collider, which is a huge circular machine that runs underground between France and Switzerland. If you straightened it out, it would measure 27km. It fires pieces of matter around in circles and smashes them against each other (*crash-land on page 67*). These collisions may release WIMPs, proving once and for all that they exist, which some scientists still argue about.

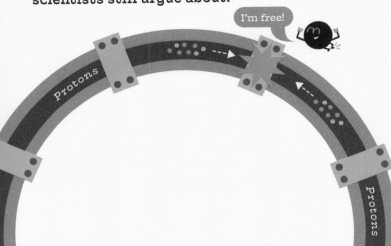

I'm free!

Protons

Protons

The Universe

You

DARK ENERGY

So, in our universe, a small part is made of stuff we can see and another larger part is made of dark matter. What about the 70% left over?

That's made of something called **DARK ENERGY**. And we have no idea what that is, other than it's the thing that is causing the universe to expand – a bit like air being blown into a football. Astronomers and physicists are busy trying to find out exactly what dark energy is made of.

Really, we have a universe made largely of stuff we can't see and don't fully understand! Well, let's keep going, and we'll hopefully learn a bit more.

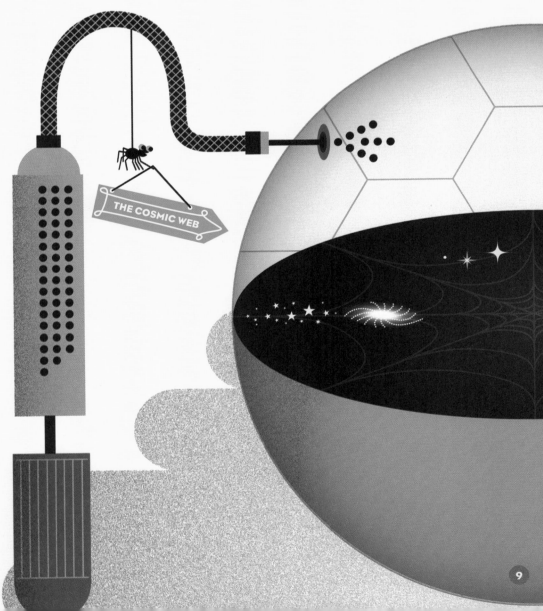

THE COSMIC WEB

STARS AND GALAXIES

Apart from dark matter and dark energy, the universe is made of things we can clearly detect and even see with our own eyes: the galaxies, stars and planets.

CITIES OF STARS

A GALAXY is a vast system of stars, like a neighbourhood. Scientists think the total number of galaxies in the universe is about two trillion (a humongously big number, more than all the grains of sand on Earth).

Our sun is in a galaxy called the MILKY WAY, along with 100 billion other stars. Most galaxies don't live on their own, though – these galactic neighbourhoods group into towns and then into cities. Our galaxy is in the Virgo supercluster, which is part of the Laniakea supercluster of 100,000 galaxies. 'Laniakea' is a Hawaiian word that means 'immense heaven'!

Galaxies come in different shapes and sizes. The Milky Way is a SPIRAL GALAXY that is shaped like a disc, with four main arms. We live on a little outpost called Orion-Cygnus.

There is a BLACK HOLE at the centre of the Milky Way. Black holes are amazing things that form when a very big star collapses in on itself. They have such strong gravity that nothing can escape them, not even light. If you fell into one you would be pulled apart and destroyed! Scientists managed to capture an incredible picture of a black hole called M87 in 2019.

The galaxies aren't staying still – in about five billion years, the Milky Way will crash into the Andromeda galaxy. But we needn't worry, as we won't be around to see it!

Sagittarius–Carina Arm

MILKY WAY NEIGHBOURHOOD

Scutum–Centaurus Arm

Norma & Outer Arm

Near 3 kpc Arm and Perseus Arm

BLACK HOLE

Maybe this is where all the leftover Milky Way chocolates go at Christmas?

CHOCO

CANDY

STARS IN OUR EYES

The STARS are made up of very hot gases, mainly hydrogen and helium (*float over to page 68*). Under heat and pressure, these gases react in a process called NUCLEAR FUSION, giving off heat and light.

When you see the light from a star, you are looking extremely far into the distance, but also back in time. It takes hundreds of years for the light from some stars to reach us, so the light you see was sent long before you were born!

When you look up into the night sky, the stars look white. But if you look with a telescope, you'll see that stars give off different colours. Stars that look red are older and cooler, and blue stars are hotter and younger.

Did you get my message to buy ice-cream?

DAME JOCELYN BELL BURNELL

Dame Jocelyn Bell Burnell is an astrophysicist from Northern Ireland who discovered a type of star called a pulsar in 1967. She wondered if the radio signal she detected was coming from aliens, so she called the signal 'LGM-1' or 'Little Green Man-1'.

Orion-Cygnus Arm

What do you mean no more Twinkle, Twinkle?

Rock Star

Stars don't really twinkle! The twinkling happens because the light from the star is changed by the Earth's turbulent atmosphere.

Guys ... my arms are getting tired.

Betelgeuse

Rigel

The Orion Constellation

JOINING THE DOTS

Thousands of years ago, humans gave stars names and drew imaginary lines between them to form **CONSTELLATIONS**. An easy one to spot is Orion, because the stars form the shape of a mythical hunter. Betelgeuse, a red star in this constellation, means 'the underarm of Orion' (I hope for Betelgeuse's sake he's wearing deodorant). Rigel, a blue star, means 'left leg of the giant'. Both of these stars were named by Arabic astronomers, who made a huge contribution to the study of stars and planets.

What's your star sign? People believed that the stars influenced humans and the natural world. This is called astrology, and some people still believe in it – but there's no science to it!

Around 4,500 stars can be counted in the night sky, and even more if you're lucky enough to have a telescope. On a clear night, look up at the stars and galaxies and be amazed!

OUR SOLAR SYSTEM

About 4.6 billion years ago, a big cloud of matter collapsed. Thanks to gravity, most of the matter came together to form a star. Planets were formed from leftover dust, which clumped together and got bigger over millions of years. Together, this star and planets formed a **solar system**.

Today, we know the sun in the sky is our very own star, and there are eight planets going around it, including the one you're sitting on as you read this. There are also moons going around these planets, and lots of asteroids, meteoroids and comets whizzing about.

Our solar system is in one of the four spiral arms of the Milky Way, orbiting the centre. Not only are you moving as the Earth rotates, and orbits the sun, but our own sun is rotating around the Milky Way, dragging the Earth and all the other planets with it. It takes our solar system 230 million years to do one complete rotation. Is your head spinning yet?

Our solar system is just one of billions! So far over 4,000 planets have been detected in the universe, but there may be up to 40 billion Earth-like planets out there – and some may well have life on them.

Believe it or not, 99.86% of all the matter in the solar system is in the sun, and most of the rest is in the planets. There are four small inner planets (Mercury, Venus, Earth and Mars) and four outer planets (Jupiter, Saturn, Uranus and Neptune). They are divided into two types: rocky, terrestrial planets and huge gas giants. There are also 181 moons, 566,000 asteroids and 3,100 comets. It might sound crowded, but most of our solar system is empty space!

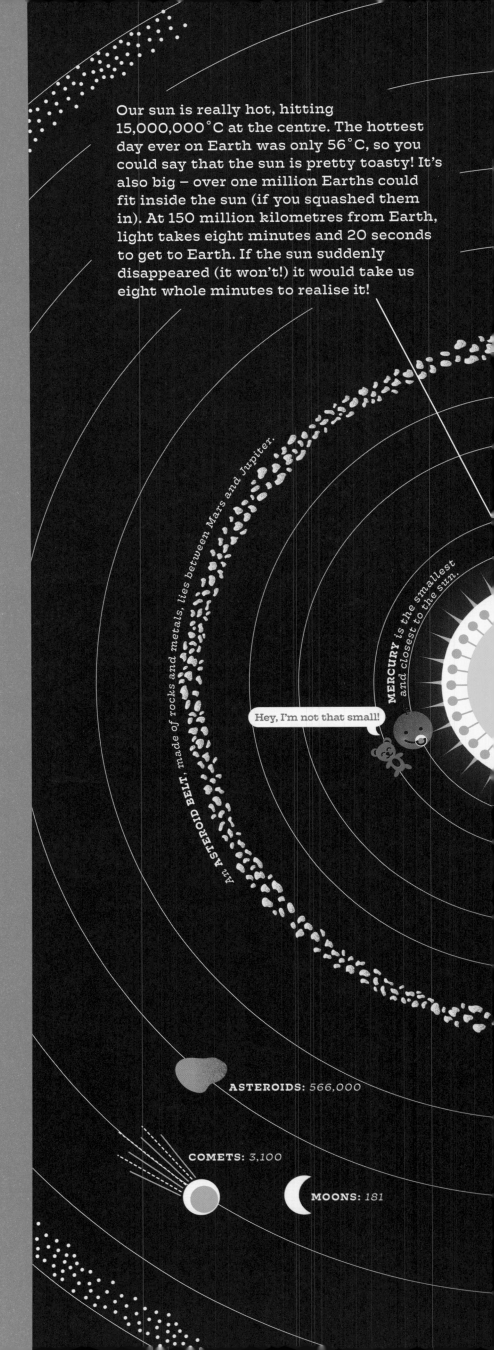

Our sun is really hot, hitting 15,000,000°C at the centre. The hottest day ever on Earth was only 56°C, so you could say that the sun is pretty toasty! It's also big – over one million Earths could fit inside the sun (if you squashed them in). At 150 million kilometres from Earth, light takes eight minutes and 20 seconds to get to Earth. If the sun suddenly disappeared (it won't!) it would take us eight whole minutes to realise it!

An ASTEROID BELT, made of rocks and metals, lies between Mars and Jupiter.

MERCURY is the smallest and closest to the sun.

Hey, I'm not that small!

ASTEROIDS: 566,000

COMETS: 3,100

MOONS: 181

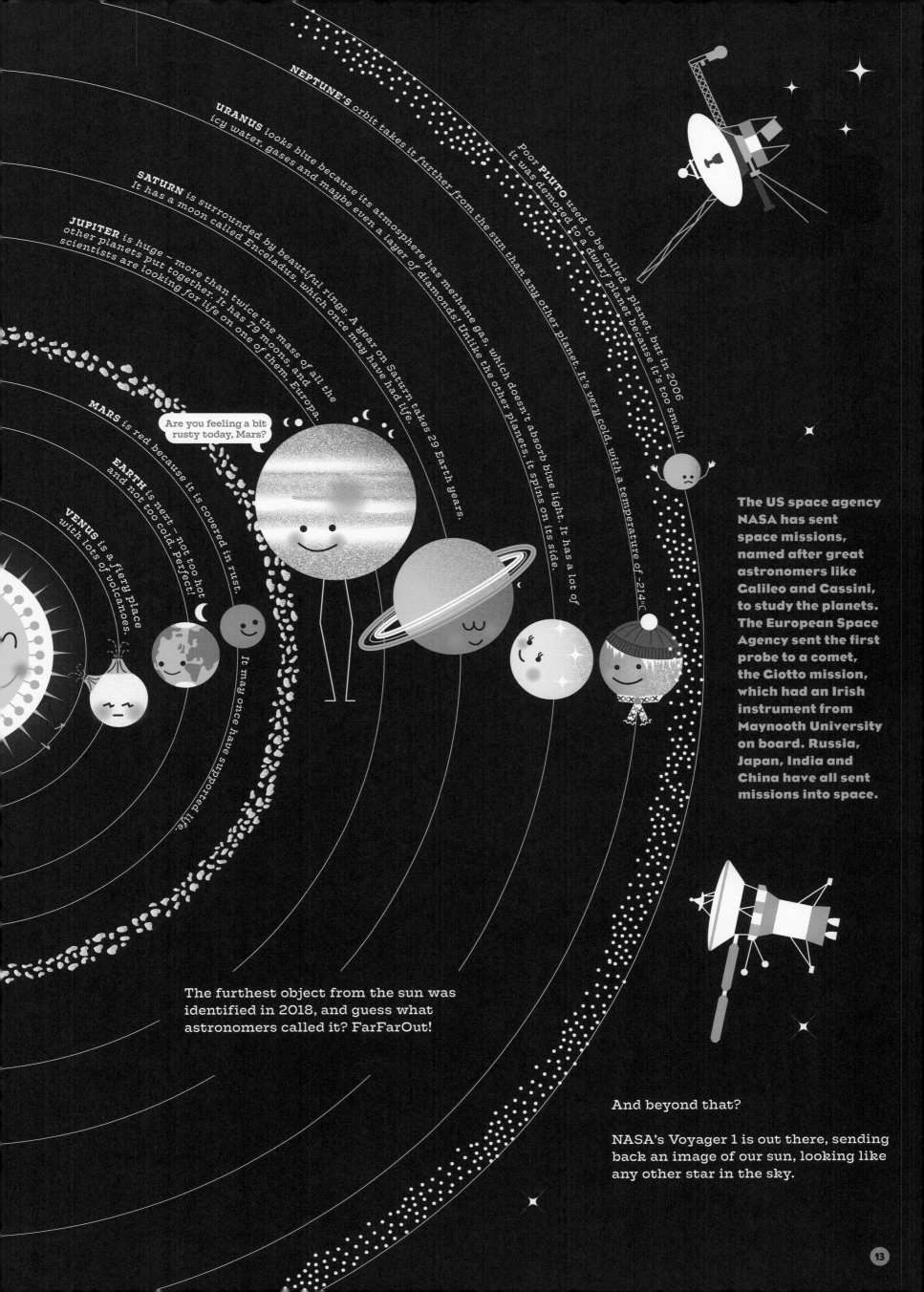

NEPTUNE'S orbit takes it further from the sun than any other planet. It's very cold, with a temperature of −214ºC.

URANUS looks blue because its atmosphere has methane gas, which doesn't absorb blue light. Unlike the other planets, it spins on its side. It has a lot of icy water, gases and maybe even a layer of diamonds!

SATURN is surrounded by beautiful rings. A year on Saturn takes 29 Earth years. It has a moon called Enceladus, which once may have had life.

JUPITER is huge – more than twice the mass of all the other planets put together. It has 79 moons, and scientists are looking for life on one of them, Europa.

MARS is red because it is covered in rust. It may once have supported life.

EARTH is next – not too hot and not too cold. Perfect!

VENUS is a fiery place with lots of volcanoes.

Poor PLUTO used to be called a planet, but in 2006 it was demoted to a dwarf planet because it's too small.

Are you feeling a bit rusty today, Mars?

The US space agency NASA has sent space missions, named after great astronomers like Galileo and Cassini, to study the planets. The European Space Agency sent the first probe to a comet, the Giotto mission, which had an Irish instrument from Maynooth University on board. Russia, Japan, India and China have all sent missions into space.

The furthest object from the sun was identified in 2018, and guess what astronomers called it? FarFarOut!

And beyond that?

NASA's Voyager 1 is out there, sending back an image of our sun, looking like any other star in the sky.

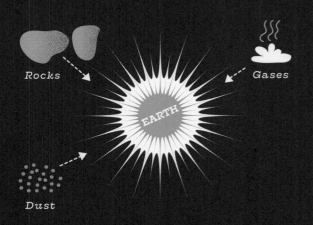

Rocks

Gases

EARTH

Dust

THE EARTH AND MOON

When Neil Armstrong walked on the moon in 1969, he put his thumb up and was able to block out the entire Earth down below. Instead of feeling very big, he said, it made him feel very small.

HOME SWEET HOME

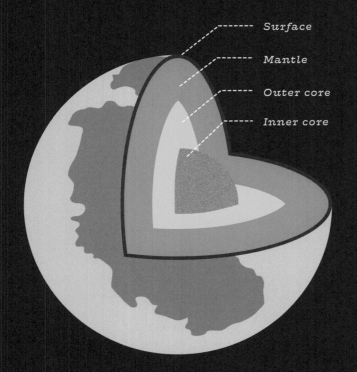

Surface

Mantle

Outer core

Inner core

Our home, the Earth, is 4.54 billion years old. It formed about 9 billion years after the Big Bang, when a cloud of dust, gases and rocks all smashed together, causing a lot of heat. This material melted into liquid rocks, and the heavier elements fell inward to form the centre of the young Earth.

This hot, heavy **INNER CORE** became solid because of the high pressure at the centre. The **OUTER CORE** is a liquid layer made of molten iron and nickel. The movement of these metals gives the Earth its magnetic field (*flow over to page 73*). The **MANTLE** is made of molten rocks called magma that move around in currents. The surface cooled to form the **CRUST**, which is the rocky surface layer that we live on.

EARLY DAYS

The early Earth was covered with volcanoes. These volcanoes released gases that formed a thin **ATMOSPHERE** around the Earth. These were mainly noxious gases like methane and hydrogen sulphide – it was like an Earth-sized stink bomb!

These volcanoes spewed up magma from the interior through cracks in the crust onto the surface. The lava then spread and hardened (*get rocking on page 20*). Eventually, a huge land mass called Pangaea was formed.

This was surrounded by oceans, which were formed from water vapour in the atmosphere, with extra water coming from comets smashing into the Earth. Over millions of years, Pangaea broke up to form the **CONTINENTS** we see today – the Americas, Africa, Europe, Asia, Australia and Antarctica.

The continents are still moving, floating around on the Earth's liquid mantle like slabs of wax sliding around on a hot plate. This is called **PLATE TECTONICS**. Sometimes they rub against each other, causing earthquakes, or crash into one another to push the crust up into mountains. The Himalayas formed when India crashed into Asia – and they're getting taller every year!

Volcanic islands are huge volcanoes which erupted on the sea floor, with their tops emerging above the sea. The Hawaiian islands are made up of five big ones, and are home to 1.4 million people!

Eurasia

North America

South America

Africa

India

Antarctica

Australia

Atmosphere

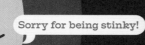

Sorry for being stinky!

Plate 1 -->

<-- Plate 2

The volcano in Honolulu is not as big as I thought ...

14

MOONING AROUND

Around 4.5 billion years ago, the Earth crashed into another planet, called Theia. Now that must have been a sight to see! This clash threw up lots of dust, which came together to form the **MOON**, and began orbiting the Earth. We know this because the moon is made of the same rocks we find in the Earth's crust, which were knocked into space by the collision and clumped together. Despite what you may have heard, the moon isn't made of cheese!

The moon is covered with **CRATERS**, which were formed when meteors crashed into the surface. It is also covered with dark 'seas' called **MARIA**. Early astronomers thought these were filled with water, but we now know they are large, dry areas of hardened rock from ancient volcanoes.

MILKY HIGHWAY

NASA sent six manned missions to the moon as part of the Apollo programme.

You are my Universe!

The moon is held in place by gravity, like two dancers swinging each other around. Although it's 384,400 km away, the moon influences the Earth, as its gravity pulls the oceans towards it, creating the tides. By coincidence, the size of the moon and its distance from the Earth means that it sometimes perfectly blots out the sun, in a **SOLAR ECLIPSE**.

Only 12 people have ever walked on the moon.

Solar Eclipse

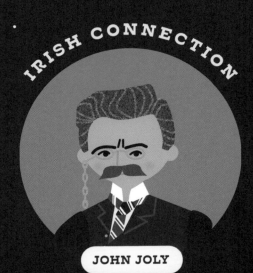

IRISH CONNECTION

JOHN JOLY

John Joly (1857-1933) was an Irish physicist and geologist. He is famous for studying the age of the Earth using radioactivity. He came up with 80-100 million years, which was far older than anyone thought at that time. He also suggested that radiotherapy would be useful to treat cancer.

THE UNIVERSE: THE FUTURE

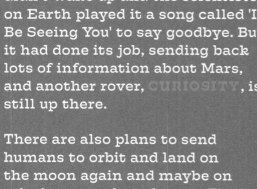

Hi, we are your 40 billion very distant cousins!

Help! We're dizzy!

Will we ever find life on other planets? This seems more and more likely, as astronomers keep finding planets going around other suns that might have the right conditions for life. They guess there are 40 billion of these (imagine, 40 billion Earth-like planets!) and surely life evolved on at least some of them?

The only trouble is, if there is life out there, it may have sent us a message long before we evolved enough to receive it. That would have been a bummer for the aliens, don't you think? Earth ghosted them because there was no one to respond. Another problem is that the universe is in a constant state of movement. Everything keeps expanding and this might mean that any life out there might be getting further and further away from us.

Meanwhile, there are plenty of space missions planned by the USA, Russia, China and Japan and also by entrepreneurs like Elon Musk with his company, SpaceX. The International Space Station continues to orbit the Earth 16 times a day – 16 sunrises and sunsets must be confusing for the astronauts. People will continue to be sent up to study how space affects humans, preparing us to go back out there.

NASA is building a new, powerful telescope to replace the Hubble telescope that's currently up there. When the James Webb telescope is sent into space, it will see further than any telescope ever before – scientists will be able to see what the universe looked like 13.4 billion years ago, soon after the Big Bang. Scientists from the Dublin Institute for Advanced Studies are involved in developing this telescope.

NASA is also planning missions to discover if there was ever life on Mars. One of their missions ended in February 2019, when NASA revealed that a Mars rover called OPPORTUNITY had sent its last digital message, which translated to 'my battery is low and it's getting dark.' Sadly, the rover didn't wake up and the scientists on Earth played it a song called 'I'll Be Seeing You' to say goodbye. But it had done its job, sending back lots of information about Mars, and another rover, CURIOSITY, is still up there.

There are also plans to send humans to orbit and land on the moon again and maybe on missions to other planets. There are even plans to set up mining and fuelling outposts on planets and the asteroid belt.

Who knows what new wonders await as we continue to explore our solar system and beyond, into the great unknown? Maybe you should become an astronomer. You'd better hurry, though, as some scientists think the universe will end in about 5 billion years ...

Ahh ... You know me, always expanding.

I see you've grown a lot!

THIS WAY

40 BILLION EARTH-LIKE PLANETS

BE A SCIENTIST!

BE A COSMOLOGIST

Go outside on a clear night, somewhere away from bright lights, and look up.

The moon is the first and most dramatic thing you can look at in the night sky. You might even be able to make out the craters and maria.

Now, look out for the stars and constellations. If the sky is very dark, after your eyes have adjusted, you'll realise that stars come in a range of colours and brightness.

You'll even be able to see planets. Mercury, Venus, Mars, Jupiter and Saturn are all visible at different times of the year. You can tell they are planets because they don't twinkle.

Try using a star chart or app and tick off what you see. If you have a pair of binoculars or a telescope, you'll see a lot more.

COSMOLOGIST

BE A ROCKET SCIENTIST

Take a 500ml plastic water bottle and tape 4 pencils to the top of the bottle to act as stabilisers.

Fill the bottle 1/3rd of the way with vinegar.

ROCKET SCIENTIST

Put 2 tablespoons of baking soda into the middle of a paper towel, roll it tight and twist the ends. Put it in the bottle and screw the cap on.

Turn the bottle upside down and stand it on the pencils. Shake it gently and stand back.

Lift off!

BE AN ASTRONOMER

When you see pictures of the solar system, everything looks like it fits perfectly. But this isn't quite how it looks in real life. Everything is much bigger and much further apart! To understand the size of the planets and their distance from the sun, you can make a model using things from your kitchen. You'll need to do this outdoors.

ASTRONOMER

Place a large beach ball on the ground – this is the sun. Now, measure the distances below with a tape measure and lay out your 'solar system'!

PLANET	OBJECT	DISTANCE TO THE SUN
MERCURY	Peppercorn	4 cm
VENUS	Pea	8 cm
EARTH	Pea	11 cm
MARS	Pea	18 cm
JUPITER	Orange	61 cm
SATURN	Tomato	98 cm
URANUS	Walnut	198 cm
NEPTUNE	Walnut	310 cm

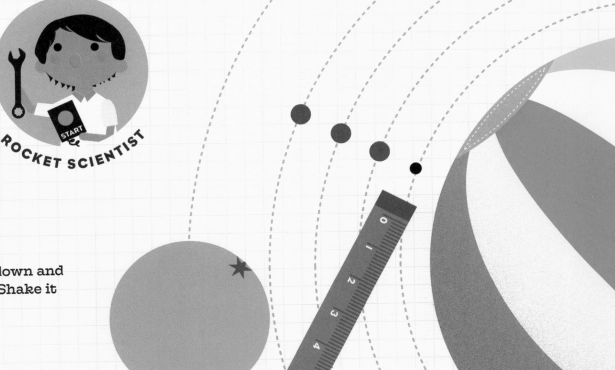

Exosphere

Thermosphere

Mesosphere

Stratosphere

Troposphere

PLANET EARTH

Now let's come right back down to Earth.

From space, our planet looks like a blue and white marble moving around the sun. As we get closer, we can make out all kinds of details.

We can see that it's a watery place, with swirling white clouds made of water vapour and large, blue oceans. The continents are covered with green forests and dry deserts, and the top and bottom of the globe are white with snow and ice.

As we get closer, we can see that the land isn't flat – it's dotted with mountains, valleys, cliffs and craters. Things are moving on the surface – animals are running, swimming, climbing and mating.

At night, networks of light shine from the cities and towns where many humans live. One of those lights might be your house. Hello! Let's take a closer look.

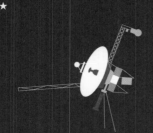

Home Sweet Home

GEOLOGY

If you dig down beneath your feet, you'll find that all sorts of rocks make up the crust of the Earth. Careful – you might hit a seam of heavy metal, or maybe even a Rolling Stone...

There are three main types of rock on Earth, and scientists called **geologists** study them.

DON'T BE AN IGNEOUS

IGNEOUS rocks form when liquid rock, or **MAGMA**, from inside the Earth's mantle cools and then hardens. Some igneous rocks harden inside the Earth and then get exposed later. Other rocks form when this liquid rock comes out of the Earth through a volcano. We call this **LAVA**, and it is very hot – at around 1100°C, it's twenty times hotter than a cup of tea! – but it cools quickly on the Earth's surface.

Like the rest of the planet, Ireland was once covered in volcanoes, so we have lots of igneous rock. The Wicklow mountains have a type of rock called granite, which contains beautiful crystals. The Giant's Causeway in Antrim is made of another igneous rock, basalt. When the lava cooled, it formed the six-sided shapes we see today.

Did you know? An igneous rock called pumice is the only rock that can float on water.

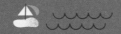

FOSSILS IN KERRY

The second type of rock is called **SEDIMENTARY**. It is formed from sand, bits of animal shells and pebbles which were pressed together into rock over millions of years.

The Burren in County Clare is a beautiful area of a sedimentary rock called limestone. An English soldier didn't like it, though – he said that there was 'not water enough to drown a man, wood enough to hang one, nor earth enough to bury him'!

Any trees around here?

This type of rock can contain **FOSSILS**, which are the remains of plants and animals that lived a long time ago, usually in the sea *(pick a bone with page 24)*. On Valentia Island, there are 365 million-year-old footprints fossilised in the rocks. These are called tetrapod (meaning four-legged) footprints and they are the oldest example of tracks made by the first creatures to leave the sea and walk on land. A momentous event in the history of life on Earth – and it's in Kerry!

META-MORPHICALLY SPEAKING

The final type of rock is called **METAMORPHIC**. This rock began its life as igneous or sedimentary rock but was changed by lots of heat or pressure. This process of change is called 'metamorphosis' (scientists love big words). Marble is an example of this type of rock. Sometimes, the heat and pressure can form crystals which mix with other chemicals, giving the rock a pretty colour. Green marble is a special type of metamorphic rock that can be found in Connemara.

LIFE AND EVOLUTION

How did life begin on this wet, rocky planet? Well, just as the Earth is the right distance from the sun – not too hot and not too cold – it seems like conditions on our young planet were like Goldilocks' porridge: just right.

COOKING WITH LUCA

Scientists called **BIOLOGISTS** have evidence of life from 3.77 billion years ago (and possibly as far back as 4.2 billion years). We know that it took at least 300 million years to appear, since the Earth was formed 4.5 billion years ago. Why did it take all this time? Well, it looks like it was a random chemical process and conditions had to be just right to cook up the first living creature.

Greetings, dear ancestor!

?

In 1871, the famous biologist Charles Darwin suggested that life might have started in a 'warm little pond' filled with chemicals, and it looks like he might have been right.

Our planet had a few special things on it that helped to jumpstart life. The surface of the young Earth was covered with **WATER**, and lots of different **CHEMICALS** were floating around in it. There was also a lot of **HEAT** from the early volcanic activity. Heat is a great way to get chemicals to change – cook some ingredients in a pot together and they will make something new. **ELECTRICITY** also helps chemicals react, and our atmosphere was filled with thunderstorms (*page 70 will shock you*). Together, these ingredients helped to start a chemical reaction which finally formed the first **CELL**.

The first living thing was tiny – you would've needed a microscope to see it (*take a cell-fie on page 52*). But that cell began to make copies of itself, which joined together to make bigger structures called **ORGANISMS**, and different cells began to do different things. All life on Earth is descended from that first cell. Biologists call it **LUCA** – the Last Universal Common Ancestor. LUCA grew and changed into different species and – to cut a very, very, very, long story short – a huge variety of species eventually appeared on Earth.

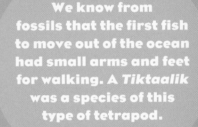

We know from fossils that the first fish to move out of the ocean had small arms and feet for walking. A *Tiktaalik* was a species of this type of tetrapod.

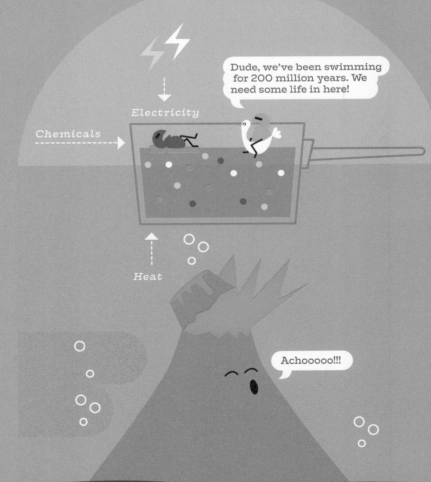

Electricity

Chemicals

Dude, we've been swimming for 200 million years. We need some life in here!

Heat

Achooooo!!!

EVOLUTION REVOLUTION

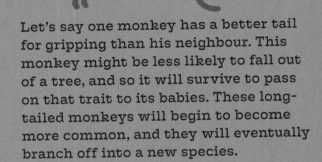

Biologists were puzzled by this. They could find thousands of species of plants and animals, often with wildly different lifestyles, shapes and sizes, but all with cells just like LUCA. Where did all these different species come from?

The answer was provided by Charles Darwin and Alfred Russell Wallace in the nineteenth century, who both came up with **NATURAL SELECTION** as the explanation. This means that the animal that is best **ADAPTED** to an environment will survive to have children.

This can happen because there is **VARIATION** between members of the same species — when two animals reproduce, their babies have different **TRAITS**, like longer claws, a shorter nose or a more flexible tail (*trait yourself on page 54*). Depending on the **ENVIRONMENT**, one animal might do better than the others and survive to pass on this trait to their children. This process became known as **EVOLUTION**.

Let's say one monkey has a better tail for gripping than his neighbour. This monkey might be less likely to fall out of a tree, and so it will survive to pass on that trait to its babies. These long-tailed monkeys will begin to become more common, and they will eventually branch off into a new species.

The huge amount of variety on Earth means that there is an animal adapted to almost every environment. But evolution hasn't stopped — life will go on evolving. I wonder what species will be on Earth one million years from now?

DINOSAURS

Life kept on evolving on the young Earth, but living things stayed small and simple for a long time. But about 540 million years ago, during what's known as the Cambrian period, there was an **explosion** of life. Living things began to become more complex, eventually leading to a huge amount of different plants and animals.

A DINO-MITE AGE

DINOSAURS lived on Earth for 150 million years because they were suited to the environment. Many species of dinosaurs have been discovered from fossilised bones (*make a fossil on page 37*). When people first found these bones, they often put them together wrong, making all sorts of strange creatures. But modern scientists are better at figuring out what these dinosaurs might have looked like. Some were reptiles – creatures like lizards – and others were more like birds.

Triceratops had three horns on its head to defend itself. It looks like the age of the dinosaurs was a vicious one!

Marshmallows, anyone?

Wow, I like the new rugby goal posts!

The biggest dinosaur found so far is called *Argentinosaurus* and it was about one-third the length of a rugby pitch.

DINO-SORE

But then, about 66 million years ago, something happened. Many dinosaurs suddenly died and eventually most of them became **EXTINCT**. The big question is ... why?

One of the best theories is an asteroid that slammed into the Earth off the coast of Mexico. This threw up so much dust into the air that the sun was blotted out. Without sunlight, many plants couldn't grow and 70% of all life on Earth died – it was like a winter that lasted for thousands of years.

This huge extinction event was bad news for the dinosaurs, but it allowed other species to have their chance. Some of those that survived all those years ago evolved into the birds we see flying around today. The ancestor of all mammals, including humans, was most likely a mouse-like creature. With the dinosaurs out of the way, these creatures could thrive and eventually lead to the age of mammals.

Dinosaurs mainly lived off plants, especially the really huge ones, but some were meat eaters. The largest of the meat eaters was *Tyrannosaurus rex*, which had huge jaws and sharp teeth, allowing it to chomp on its prey – most likely the plant-eating dinosaurs.

The smallest, *Microraptor*, was only the size of a baseball bat.

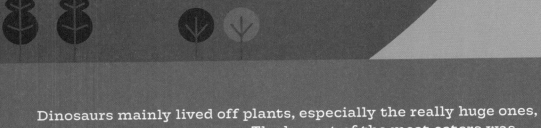

Other species like *Stegosaurus* had sharp plates on its back to stop it being eaten, but its brain was only the size of a ping pong ball. The plates used to turn red to warn off predators!

25

ANIMALS

Although they only make up 0.36% of life on Earth, animals dominate our planet. But what exactly is an animal? Well, animals move, don't they? But ... so do plants. Animals have fur – but so do some plants! Hmm, we'll have to think about this a bit. We can say that an animal is a living thing that ...

... **feeds** on plants or other animals

... and that has a **nervous system**

... that can **respond** to its environment.

Quite a precise definition, but an important one.

ADAPTING ANIMALS

Animals are grouped into two main types depending on whether they have a backbone – the vertebrates – or not – the invertebrates. You're a vertebrate, and a snail is an invertebrate. As many as ten million species of animals have been found.

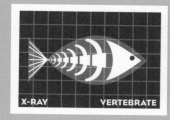
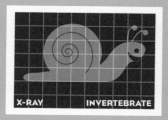

WARM-BLOODED animals, like birds and mammals, can generate their own body heat from food. We humans keep our body temperature at 37°C. **COLD-BLOODED** animals, like lizards, can't do this and their body temperature rises and falls depending on their surroundings. Some fish live in water that's almost freezing, and they hardly move at all.

MY TOP TEN ANIMAL FACTS

1. A shrimp's heart is in its head.
2. A snail can sleep for three years.
3. Slugs have four noses.
4. It takes a sloth two weeks to digest its dinner.
5. Nearly 3% of ice in the Antarctic is penguin urine.
6. Octopuses can't fart.
7. Frogs can't vomit, but they can eject their entire stomach if they eat poison.
8. Cats meow not to talk to each other, but to get the attention of humans.
9. Wombat poop is cube-shaped.
10. A naked mole rat's front teeth can work together like a pair of chopsticks.

Animals come in a huge range of sizes. The largest animal is the blue whale, which can grow to 30 metres – longer than two buses. The smallest animal is called a mesozoan and it's only 50 cells big, and it can only be seen with a microscope.

Of all the different species of animals, insects are the most impressive. Incredibly, they make up half of all the animals on Earth. Beetles alone have 350,000 species, and an entomologist has catalogued them all (must be a real fan of The Beatles).

Animals have **ADAPTED** to live almost anywhere on Earth. Polar bears can live in the frozen wasteland of the Arctic because they have a layer of fat under their fur, while scorpions can survive in the unbearable (at least for us) heat of the desert by burrowing into the cooler sand.

Scientists think there are five organisms we couldn't live without. One of them is bees, because they pollinate the plants we eat. Can you guess the other four? They might surprise you!

primates, bats, fungi and plankton

THE EQUATION OF LIFE

For all animals, life is always a struggle. They must eat to survive while trying not to be eaten themselves, and they must also reproduce. These three things drive much of animal behaviour.

For example, tigers need to sleep for 20 hours a day. I bet you think that's just being lazy, but they are saving their energy in case a nice tasty antelope comes along. There wouldn't be much point in you using up energy to walk downstairs for a bowl of cereal if there wasn't enough energy in it to replace what you use up in the walk.

All of life is an equation, and animals are very good at doing this calculation.

IRISH CONNECTION

CYNTHIA LONGFIELD

Cynthia Longfield (1896–1991) from County Cork was an explorer and expert on dragonflies who became known as Madam Dragonfly. She worked at the British Museum and travelled around the world collecting and discovering new species. Two species have even been named after her.

HUMAN EVOLUTION

Now we've made it all the way up to us – humans. Or, to give us our proper name, **Homo sapiens**, which means 'wise human'. We only make up about 0.01% of life on Earth, but our activities certainly have the biggest influence on the planet.

But where did we come from? Well, like all animals, we evolved from earlier life forms according to the law of evolution by natural selection. Our early ancestors would have been reptile-like, then fish-like, then mammals, then primates (something like a chimpanzee) and then on to us, all driven by the **survival of the fittest** over millions and millions of years.

15,000 YEARS AGO

Americas

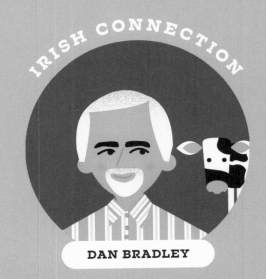
Dan Bradley is an Irish geneticist who uses DNA analysis to study the origins of the Irish people in Europe. He has also uncovered when humans domesticated cattle.

Around 100,000 years ago, a small group left Africa and moved to the Middle East. About 70,000 years ago, some of us moved to Asia, and from there to Australia, and later to the Americas. 40,000 years ago we moved into Europe and we reached Ireland about 12,000 years ago (although we would have gotten there sooner if an Ice Age hadn't gotten in the way - *cool off on page 34*).

We used our inventiveness to survive as we moved into the colder northern areas, wearing animal skins and using fire. We also discovered **AGRICULTURE** in the Middle East and learned to **DOMESTICATE** animals. This gave us a big advantage and we started to build towns and cities.

When our ancestors moved into Europe, something interesting happened. They met a different species called the Neanderthals, who were very like us. Our ancestors mated with them, resulting in a new type of human.

Today, we all carry some Neanderthal DNA. They gave us genes to make our nails, hair, skin and immune systems stronger.

Finally, we went on the move again. Our inventiveness led us to build ships and we travelled from Europe to the Americas and Australia and met our long-lost cousins. Our family was finally reunited. This might be the greatest story ever: the human journey began 200,000 years ago and is still continuing today.

But if the whole story of life on Earth was shown on a clock over 24 hours, we appear very recently, at just one minute and 17 seconds to midnight — we came late to the party. And the party might well go on without us.

THE HUMAN STORY

Homo sapiens emerged in Africa at least 300,000 years ago. But what made us special as a species? What made us stand out? Compared to other species of primates, we were hugely inventive. We used **TOOLS** in all kinds of interesting ways, like to cut and to defend ourselves. We also did things like bury our dead and artistic activities like painting on cave walls. We discovered how to make **FIRE** which we could use to stay warm and cook food, helping us feed our big brains.

Fish   Tiktaalik   Mammals   Primates   Humans

PLANTS

Life on Earth belongs in one of five kingdoms: plants, animals, fungi, bacteria and protists (which includes everything left over!) Scientists have recently come up with an estimate for the combined weight of life on Earth: 550 gigatonnes. An average car weighs 1 tonne, so life weighs the same as 550 billion cars.

Bacteria make up 70 gigatonnes, and fungi 12 gigatonnes (there's not mush-room for them). Animals (including us) make up 2 gigatonnes. All the humans on Earth combined weigh in at 0.06 gigatonnes – pretty puny. But 450 gigatonnes are plants!

CAN YOU BE-LEAF IT?

Plants are living things that use **PHOTOSYNTHESIS**, which means that they can take energy from sunlight. They also take in nutrients from the soil and water through their roots. It's a pretty good trick – plants use these ingredients to make more of themselves.

Leaves are the factories of the plant. A chemical called chlorophyll in leaves absorbs sunlight and gives plants their green colour.

The air is made up of lots of different gases, but two important ones are **CARBON DIOXIDE** and **OXYGEN**. We need to have the right balance of these gases for many creatures – including humans – to live. Humans breathe in oxygen and breathe out carbon dioxide, but luckily, plants do it the other way around. They take in carbon dioxide and release oxygen. This means they can lower the carbon dioxide in the air (*but see what happens without them on page 34*).

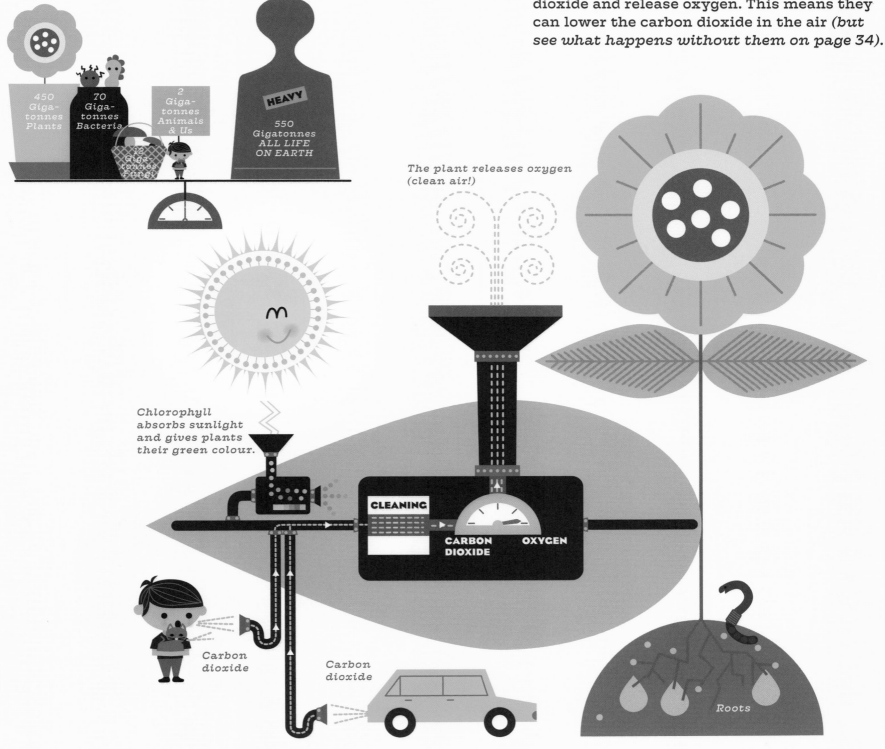

450 Giga-tonnes Plants

70 Giga-tonnes Bacteria

2 Giga-tonnes Animals & Us

12 Giga-tonnes Fungi

HEAVY

550 Gigatonnes ALL LIFE ON EARTH

The plant releases oxygen (clean air!)

Chlorophyll absorbs sunlight and gives plants their green colour.

CLEANING

CARBON DIOXIDE

OXYGEN

Carbon dioxide

Carbon dioxide

Roots

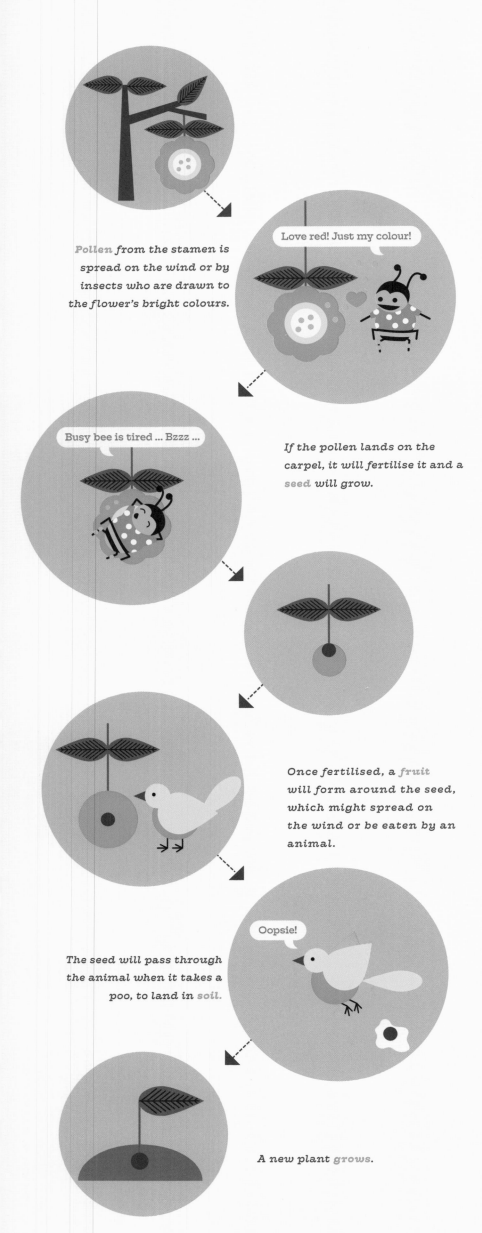

Pollen from the stamen is spread on the wind or by insects who are drawn to the flower's bright colours.

Love red! Just my colour!

Busy bee is tired ... Bzzz ...

If the pollen lands on the carpel, it will fertilise it and a seed will grow.

Once fertilised, a fruit will form around the seed, which might spread on the wind or be eaten by an animal.

Oopsie!

The seed will pass through the animal when it takes a poo, to land in soil.

A new plant grows.

FLOWER POWER

Flowering plants make up 80% of all plant life. The flowers aren't just there to look and smell pretty – they're needed for reproduction, which means making new versions of themselves (*like humans do on page 50*).

Flowers contain a female part, called the **CARPEL**, and a male part, called the **STAMEN**. The male part of the flower produces **POLLEN**, which fertilises the female part. Achoo!

Are you a boy or a girl?

I'm both!

Me too!

ONE, TWO, TREE

TREES cover about 30% of Earth's land surface. **DECIDUOUS** trees lose their leaves in autumn as the days get shorter and the temperature drops. The colour changes because the plants use up the chlorophyll in the leaves, exposing the colours that are already there, like yellow and red. The leaf then falls off the tree, to be recycled in the soil. **EVERGREEN** trees keep their leaves all year round.

Some plants have evolved to defend themselves from being eaten. Cacti use sharp spikes, nettles have stinging cells, and others use poison!

Apart from providing food and oxygen, plants are an important source of medicine, and we use plants to mark important events, like weddings and funerals. It's simple: without plants we would not be here.

Let's have a look overleaf, shall we?

IRISH CONNECTION

ELLEN HUTCHINS

Ellen Hutchins (1785–1815) was an Irish botanist who identified hundreds of plants in the Bantry Bay area of Cork. She was interested in seaweeds and lichens, and many plants are named after her.

POLAR habitats are found at the north and south poles. The coldest temperature ever recorded was −89.2°C in Antarctica. Life is scarce in polar regions. Trees can't grow because they can't send down roots into the frozen ground, but small plants like mosses and shrubs can grow because their roots are much shorter. Birds like penguins have very short feathers that trap a layer of air to keep them warm.

Summer at last!

DESERTS are very dry and hot. They can get less than 25cm of rain in a year, and sometimes that falls in one big rain shower. The hottest temperature on Earth was recorded in Death Valley, California, where it hit 56°C. When the sun goes down, deserts can get very cold at night. But plants and animals can survive even these harsh conditions – cacti store water in their stems for times of drought, and fennec foxes only come out at night to hunt when it's cool.

WELCOME TO
DEATH VALLEY
THE PLACE YOU'LL
NEVER WANT TO LEAVE

HABITATS

The place where a species of plant or animal lives is called a **habitat**. The Earth is covered with lots of different types of habitats, and life has evolved to survive almost anywhere.

MOUNTAINS have a range of habitats. Deciduous forests grow at lower levels, and evergreen forests grow higher up, where it's cooler. The highest mountain on Earth is Mount Everest, which is 8,848m tall – that's 5,000 people standing on top of each other! Humans couldn't survive for long in these high, cold places, but animals like grizzly bears hibernate in the winter and come out when it gets warmer.

I'm an extremophile!

Himalayan Jumping Spider

Some organisms have evolved to survive high levels of heat, cold, salt and even radiation. We call these extremophiles.

RAINFORESTS grow in the tropics around the equator and are full of species. Life loves the rainforests, because it is warm and wet. They have wonderful plants that give us things like chocolate (from the cocoa tree) and flowers with gorgeous names like lobster-claw and the passion fruit flower. Half of the world's species live in rainforests, from anacondas to wolf spiders.

There are several types of AQUATIC habitats, including freshwater rivers and salty oceans. Each is filled with life. The Amazon is the longest river in the world, flowing for 6,400 km from the Andes mountains to the Atlantic Ocean. Snails, worms, frogs, turtles, alligators and many types of fish live in freshwater habitats. The largest animal of them all, the blue whale, is an ocean dweller.

IRISH CONNECTION

MAUDE DELAP

Maude Delap (1866–1953) was a marine biologist from County Donegal who was the first person to breed jellyfish in captivity.

Oak

Ash

Elm

Beech

In TEMPERATE regions like Ireland, it never gets too hot or cold. Oak, elm, ash and beech trees all grow in temperate habitats. Many species love these forests, including squirrels, hedgehogs and many species of birds.

Ireland has other special habitats of its very own, like bogs, sea cliffs and marram dunes. A lot of species in Ireland are in danger, though, like the red squirrel, pygmy shrew and bank vole.

All around the world, humans are changing natural habitats and unwanted predators are wiping plants and animals out. Life is tough, and it will probably continue in some form, no matter what we do. But what would the world be like without trees, plants, bears and bees?

33

Carbon dioxide

When we travel, our cars, planes and trucks burn even more fuel and release **CARBON DIOXIDE**.

At the same time, **DEFORESTATION** is knocking down trees to make room for homes or farming land. Forests are the lungs of the Earth, so this is suffocating us (*see why on page 30*).

Methane gas

We farm huge amounts of cattle for food. Cow farts and burps are full of **METHANE**, another greenhouse gas.

CLIMATE CHANGE

Over the past 650,000 years, there have been seven **ice ages**, when the Earth's temperature dropped and ice covered the globe. These were largely caused by changes in the amount of heat coming from the sun.

But over the past few hundred years, scientists have noticed that the average temperature of the Earth has RISEN at ten times the expected rate. And the reason? Human activity.

Our factories, homes, cars and planes burn FOSSIL FUELS like coal, oil and gas, which release carbon dioxide and other gases into the air (*learn about green fuels on page 70*).

These gases trap the sun's heat, just like the glass in a hot greenhouse keeps the inside warm. We call them GREENHOUSE GASES, and we have too much of them in our atmosphere.

All of this is making poor Planet Earth sick: it has a temperature, which has risen by 1.2°C over the past hundred years. This is enough to speed up the melting of the polar ice caps and glaciers in high mountains. It's causing coral reefs in our oceans to die off. It's also the reason for harsher weather conditions around the world, with storms and floods becoming more severe. Climate change is already costing billions of euros in damage.

More importantly, it is already affecting people. The countries that will be most affected are the poorer countries, the ones that didn't cause the problem. They will be more prone to flooding and agricultural disasters, leading to future poverty. It might also mean that there will be climate refugees: millions of people moving to find shelter or food.

Climate change is also threatening many species. Human activity has already caused the EXTINCTION of 83% of mammals and 50% of plants. Every day, plants and animals are dying off for ever. Life is one big connected web, and there's no knowing what will happen if a certain species becomes extinct. Right now, we are facing one of the biggest threats to life on Earth. But what can we do?

FIGHTING FOR THE PLANET

Are you fighting climate change? Try this quiz ...

How do you get to school?
A. I go by car. I enjoy the traffic! (+1)
B. I take the bus with my friends. (+3)
C. I walk or cycle to keep myself fit. (+5)
Bonus: I have to go by car, but I pick up my friends. (+2)

Time for lunch. What do you do?
A. I buy my lunch ... and throw the wrappers in the yard. (+1)
B. I bring it from home, wrapped up in plastic. (+3)
C. I bring my own lunchbox and drinking bottle and recycle the rest. (+5)

It's the weekend and you've got pocket money!
A. I buy lots of new things. Have to keep up with the fashions! (+1)
B. I buy something I really need ... plus a little treat. (+3)
C. I buy second-hand clothes or things made from recycled materials. (+5)
Bonus: I also mend my old things instead of buying something new. (+2)

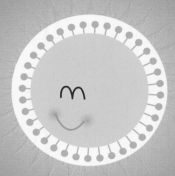

Brrr – the Irish summer is here and it's raining! What do you do?
A. I put on the heating, quick! (+1)
B. I close all the windows, quick! (+3)
C. I put on my jumper and close the windows, quick! (+5)
Bonus: I also turn all my appliances off at the wall. Say no to standby. (+2)

Is all this quizzing making you hungry?
A. I get a takeaway burger, maybe a fizzy drink, some crisps ... mmm. (+1)
B. I buy my own ingredients and recycle the packaging. (+3)
C. I grow my own food and compost the leftovers. (+5)
Bonus: I cork the bums of any cows I see. Only joking! I try to eat less meat. (+2)

What are you going to do when you finish this book?
A. Make greener choices in my life and tell everyone I know to do the same. (+5)
B. Write to my local politician and ask them what they are doing about climate change. (+5)
C. Study the science behind climate change and try to think of solutions myself (+5)
Bonus: Do nothing. It'll be grand! (−5)

If you score **below 15,** you're a rootin' tootin' pollutin' cowboy! Make some changes – quick!
If you score **between 18 and 25**, you're doing OK – but you could do better. Time to train up.
If you score **over 25**, you're a green Cú Chulainn! Now spread the word.

Dear Pol I. Tician,

My name is _____ and I am a scientist. I want to know what you are doing about climate change. Saving the planet matters much more to me because I am young and you are old. If you don't do your job, me and my friends will use THE INTERNET to tell everyone not to vote for you in the next election.

Very seriously yours,

_____

Remember the 5 Rs!
REFUSE – say no to disposable
REDUCE – do you really need to buy that?
REUSE – use it again and again
RECYCLE – clean, separate and recycle
ROT – compost your scraps

PLANET EARTH: THE FUTURE

What scientists are most concerned about when it comes to the future of the Earth is climate change. Habitats, plants and animals are all being affected. Scientists think that global climate change is likely to harm millions of people because of drought, famine and flooding.

If temperatures keep rising and oxygen levels drop, life on Earth might be in trouble. Over millions of years, animals might be driven away from the sun towards the poles, and maybe even underground. The surface of the Earth would become a desert, and life would mainly be found in the oceans. But eventually, sea life would disappear too.

In the past, life has almost been wiped out altogether. This was caused by natural changes in the climate, meteorites and even gamma rays from a distant galaxy. These events were known as mass extinctions, and more of them are likely to happen in the future. The trouble is, we humans are causing mass extinctions right now, mainly because of what we're doing to the environment. This has to stop!

But as long as life isn't wiped out, it will keep on evolving and changing in the future – nothing stands still on Planet Earth.

BE A SCIENTIST!

BE A ZOOLOGIST

You'd love your own wormery, wouldn't you?

Fill a large jar with a thick layer of damp soil and a thin layer of sand. Repeat, but leave some space at the top of the jar.

Collect three worms in your garden or park and put them on top – gently!

Add some dead leaves and vegetable peelings to the jar.

Poke some airholes in the lid, close the jar, and leave it in a dark place.

After two weeks take a look. The worms will have mixed up the soil and sand and made tunnels. Now return the worms to your garden!

ZOOLOGIST

BE A PALAEONTOLOGIST

Add a cup of salt, two cups of flour and ¾ cup of water to a bowl. Mix well and make a dough.

Press a dinosaur toy into the dough to leave an imprint or try different shapes for footprints – add as many toes as you like.

Bake at 200°C for 45 minutes. You've made a 'fossil'.

TIP: Put a trail of footprints into the dough, and you'll have a fossil like the tetrapod footprints in Kerry!

PALAEONTOLOGIST

BE A VOLCANOLOGIST

I bet you didn't know you could make a volcano in your kitchen!

Place two tablespoons of baking soda in the bottom of a glass. Add a few drops of food colouring and put the glass in a saucepan.

Quickly pour in ½ cup of vinegar. Watch for the eruption!

TIP: You could make a volcano shape out of a plastic bottle. Try adding washing-up liquid, salt or sugar to the mixture. What happens to the eruption?

VOLCANOLOGIST

COLOUR

COLOUR

BE A CLIMATOLOGIST

Fill a clear baking dish about ⅓ full of cold water and add a few drops of blue food colouring.

Add two cups of ice to the cold water and stir. While the ice is melting, boil about four cups of water. Add red food colouring to the hot water.

CLIMATOLOGIST

Once both sets of water and dye are ready, gently pour some of the hot water into a corner of the baking dish.

Then, watch as currents form right before your eyes as the hot water pushes through the cold water. Eventually, the water and colours will mix to create lukewarm water. This also happens in the ocean. (But it doesn't turn purple!)

TIP: Put a stone shaped like Ireland in the middle of the dish and watch the current flow around it.

THE HUMAN BODY

And so, we come to us – to you, me and all humans. We are the masters of the universe. Or are we?

We only make up a tiny fraction of life on Earth. But we're very smart, and we can do science, so I guess that makes us special. But then again, we used to keep rocks as pets, invented weapons to kill each other and watch reality TV ...

But we are special. Our bodies can do incredible things – they can run, jump, swim, think and imagine. They can turn tiny chemicals into complicated things like bones, skin and the squishy thing we call a brain where our thoughts live. Even more amazingly, two people together can make a whole new person. And perhaps best of all, if something breaks down, our bodies can repair themselves.

Let's look a little more closely at the glorious thing that is your body, a well-oiled machine for life like no other.

THE SKELETON

You're still growing as you read this. You are getting taller and taller, and this is because your bones are getting longer.

Even though your skull is tough, if you bang your head, your brain can shake and hit the inside of your skull. This can cause long-term damage, so always have a head injury checked out.

DEM BONES DEM BONES

Your **SKELETON** is the biggest structure in your body, made up of 206 bones. When you were a baby, though, you had 270 bones. Did you leave some in school?! (You didn't. Some of the bones fuse together as you grow towards being an adult.)

Bones protect and help different parts of your body.

Your skeleton is helped by **LIGAMENTS** (that link bone to bone) and **TENDONS** (that link bone to muscle).

The middle of your bones is filled with **MARROW**, where blood cells are made – bet you didn't know your bones were factories for your blood!

If you break a bone, it will knit back together. The body is great at healing bones, especially when you're young. This doesn't mean you have a licence to go breaking your leg, though!

Without your skeleton you would be like a lump of jelly, spread over the floor. And that wouldn't be a nice sight, now would it?

About 40% of your bones are made of a hard mineral that contains the metal calcium. That's why you need calcium in your diet.

Two bones meet at a **JOINT**, like your elbows, knees and knuckles.

The popping noise when you crack your knuckles comes from bubbles bursting in the fluid surrounding the joint.

Your **SKULL** is very important because it protects your brain, which is very delicate. But evolution made sure you have your very own crash helmet!

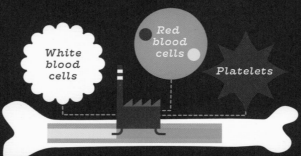

White blood cells

Red blood cells

Platelets

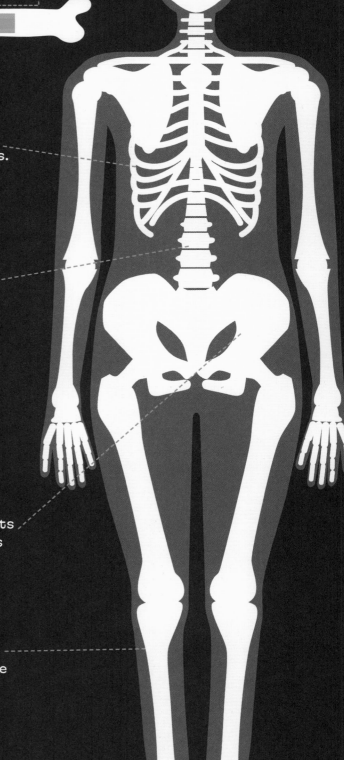

Your **RIBS** protect your heart and lungs.

Your **SPINE** helps you stand up and supports your head.

Your **PELVIS** protects your organs and lets you move around.

Your **ARM** and **LEG** bones help you move your limbs.

MUSCLING IN

Muscles are made of a type of flexible **TISSUE**, and they control all movement in your body. There are around 650 different muscles in your body.

SKELETAL MUSCLES help you move around, and you can control what they do. Many come in pairs, like the biceps and triceps in your arm – when one gets longer, the other gets shorter and this lets you bend your arm.

Inside your body are **SMOOTH MUSCLES**. These work without you thinking about them, like the muscles that help push food through your body.

Your heart has a very special and strong type called **CARDIAC MUSCLE**, which pumps blood all around your body.

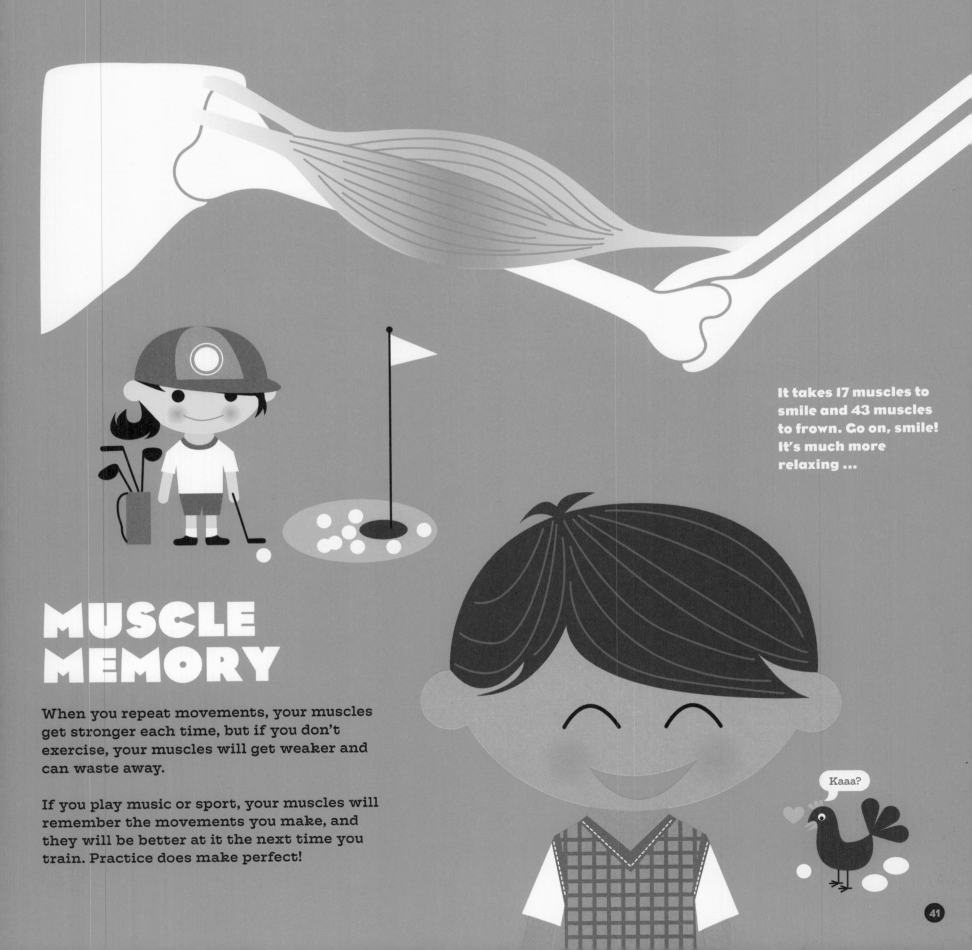

It takes 17 muscles to smile and 43 muscles to frown. Go on, smile! It's much more relaxing ...

MUSCLE MEMORY

When you repeat movements, your muscles get stronger each time, but if you don't exercise, your muscles will get weaker and can waste away.

If you play music or sport, your muscles will remember the movements you make, and they will be better at it the next time you train. Practice does make perfect!

Kaaa?

THE BRAIN

As you read this sentence, all kinds of things are happening in a big, pink-grey mushy thing in your head. It is crackling away, alive with electricity. It's your **brain**, easily the most complex thing we know of in the universe.

The **CEREBRUM** is the biggest part of the brain. It has lots of wrinkles. The back of the cerebrum deals with vision, while other parts control movement, hearing, language and touch.

Your memories are stored in a part called the **HIPPOCAMPUS**. When you remember that movie you watched last week, you're activating that memory.

The **CEREBELLUM** is at the back of the brain. Its job is to control movement, like when you write with a pen or ride your bicycle.

When you sleep at night, lots of interesting things happen in your brain. Tiny channels open up to clean up after a hard day of thinking.

The **SPINAL CORD** runs down your spine and sends out neurons to all parts of your body in a big network of communication.

The **BRAIN STEM** is deep inside your brain and controls all the things that keep your body going without you thinking about them, like your heart beating.

The **AMYGDALA** is the part of the brain where your emotions are. When you are angry, sad or happy (which we all feel from time to time) the amygdala shouts, cries or laughs.

THE BRAIN'S RELAY RACE

The brain is like a central computer that controls the body. It uses a network called the **NERVOUS SYSTEM** to pass messages to and from different parts of the body. In your brain, there are two main types of cells: **NEURONS** and **GLIAL** cells. Neurons are where all the action in the brain happens and the glial cells provide support.

Incredibly, there are over 80 billion neurons in your brain – almost the same number of stars that are in the Milky Way.

Neurons are made up of two parts: the main **CELL BODY** and long, dangly bits called **AXONS**. These reach out and almost touch nearby neurons, forming a connection called a **SYNAPSE**.

An electrical current runs down the axon, and it causes chemicals called **NEUROTRANSMITTERS** to be released. These jump across the synapse, hit off the next neuron, and trigger an electrical current to move down to the next neuron – a bit like a really fast relay race.

This is what happens when you tell your hand to grab a door handle. The signal moves down neurons from your brain into your muscles, which twitch – and your arm moves.

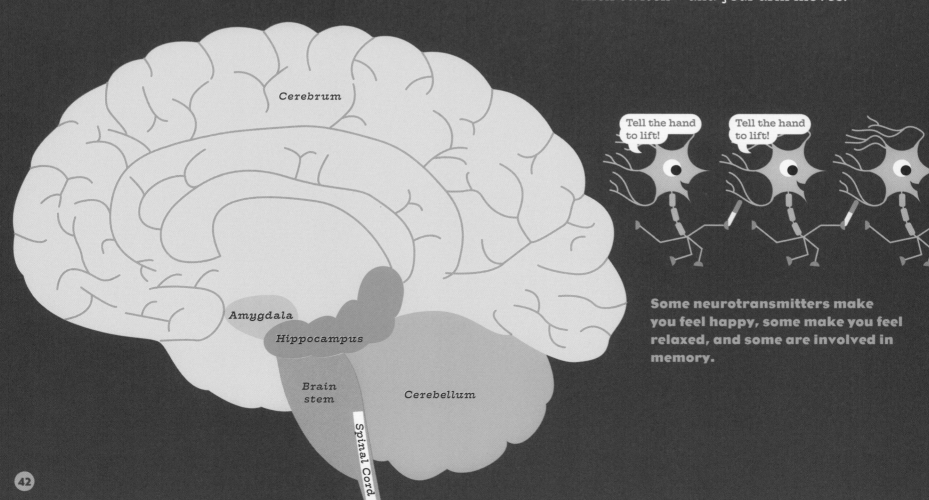

Cerebrum

Amygdala

Hippocampus

Brain stem

Cerebellum

Spinal Cord

Tell the hand to lift!

Tell the hand to lift!

Some neurotransmitters make you feel happy, some make you feel relaxed, and some are involved in memory.

THE FIVE SENSES

One of the most amazing things about your brain is how it can understand signals from the outside world.

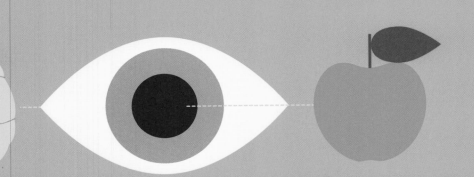

When you **SEE** an apple, light bounces off it, goes into your eye, and is focused onto the back of your eye by your pupil. This sends an electrical message to your brain, which creates the image of an apple. You remember that apples are tasty, so your brain tells you that it looks delicious.

You pick it up and it **FEELS** smooth. When you touch something, sensors in your skin send signals to your brain to decide what it is you're touching. We can tell if something is cold, hot, smooth or rough. We can also sense pressure, pain and feel itchy.

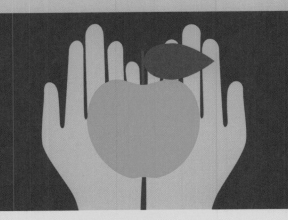

Then you **SMELL** the sweet, fruity smell. Tiny chemicals are detected by your nose and they send a message to your brain. Scientists have shown that we can smell up to ... wait for it ... a trillion different chemicals!

You bite into the apple and **HEAR** a crunching noise. The noise goes into your ear and hits off your eardrum, which vibrates. Tiny bones send the noise to a special nerve which sends a signal to your brain.

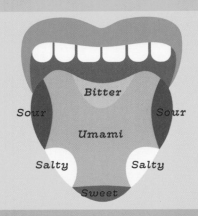

Then you **TASTE** the apple as the flavour explodes in your mouth. Your tongue has tiny bumps called taste buds that send messages to your brain. There are five flavours: sweet, sour, salty, bitter and umami (found in things like soy sauce – umami makes Chinese food taste great).

All your senses are triggered when you eat an apple! *(Which can be useful – see page 82.)*

We are best buds, taste buds.

43

THE DIGESTIVE SYSTEM

Has all that talk of apples made you hungry? Hunger is a strange sensation in your stomach, but your brain is also saying 'go get something to eat.' You'd better listen!

Once you find some food, the process of **DIGESTION** begins.

Your **LIVER** takes these nutrients and decides what to do with them.

I'll keep working as long as I liver.

Liver

Enzymes

Pancreas   Enzymes

Stomach

Special chemicals in your saliva called **ENZYMES** help soften the food.

You first **CHEW** the food with your teeth to break it up. You have 32 teeth – the incisors at the front are for biting, canines are for tearing, and the molars at the back are for grinding.

Salivary Gland

Salivary Gland

Oesophagus

When you swallow, muscles push the mushy food down your **OESOPHAGUS**.

Once the food hits your **STOMACH**, more enzymes really get to work, breaking down the proteins in your food. There is also acid in your stomach which kills bacteria and loosens the food.

DID I EAT THAT?

Animals that eat only meat are carnivores while those that eat plants are herbivores. Humans aren't very fussy, though: we can eat meat or plants, so we are known as **OMNIVORES**. In a healthy diet, a bit of everything is important – lots of fruit and vegetables with only a little meat (although some humans choose to eat none at all). We also need **VITAMINS**, like vitamin D, which keeps our bones strong, and **MINERALS**, like iron for healthy blood. Most of all, we need to be careful that we don't eat too much and move too little!

You would last three weeks without food, but only three days without water. Our bodies are 60% water and we need to keep topping it up.

Water and nutrients to the blood

Bloodstream

Your **KIDNEYS** remove any waste products and put them into urine, which is stored in your **BLADDER**.

Small Intestine

The watery food now enters your **SMALL INTESTINE**, where more enzymes, made by the **LIVER** and **PANCREAS**, break the food down into tiny pieces. The nutrients are absorbed into your body with great gurgling noises.

Large Intestine

Anything left over enters your **LARGE INTESTINE**, where more absorption can happen.

Any waste becomes **FAECES**, or poo, which is brown because it contains dead red blood cells.

Appendix

Kidneys

It takes around three days for all this to happen. For some animals, digestion takes much longer: 16 days for a green iguana, because they don't need to go to the toilet very often.

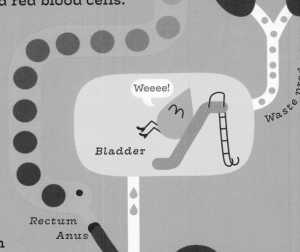

Weeee!

Bladder

Waste products

Rectum
Anus

The poo then enters the **RECTUM** and on out through the anus. Make sure you flush!

What's for dinner, Mum?

Poo-tatoes.

Wee *Poo*

There are billions of bacteria in your digestive system – they make up 3% of your body weight! Some of them help with digestion, but they also make poo smell nasty. This is to stop you eating it. The poo of some animals, like mice, has more leftover nutrients so they will eat their own poo.

THE CIRCULATORY SYSTEM

Every car needs oil. It keeps the engine clean and keeps it running smoothly. **Blood** works like that for our bodies, but it's even better than oil, because ...

- It carries oxygen and nutrients all over our bodies.
- It also moves heat around our bodies to keep us warm.
- In just one day, blood travels about 19,000 km around your body.
- If you were to drain all the blood from your body (not a good idea) it would come to about 4 litres.
- It can help you get better when you get sick.

And all in that red stuff that leaks out when you cut yourself!

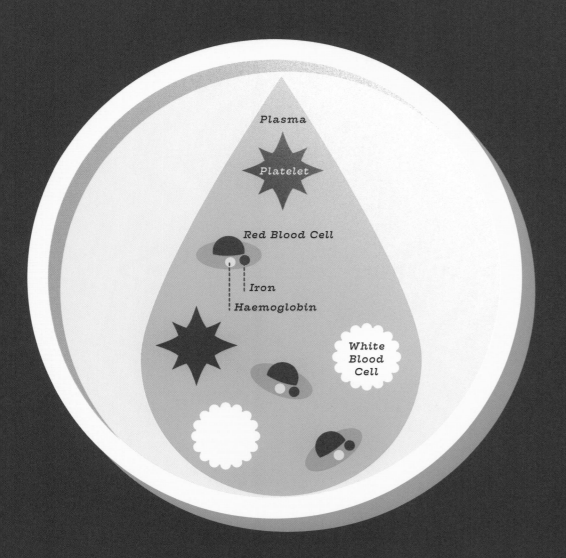

Many people donate blood to others who need it after an accident or illness. There are four types of blood – A, B, AB and O – and these can be either positive or negative. O positive is the most common group in Ireland, and AB negative is the least common.

BLOODY BITS

Let's have a look at a drop of blood – we'll need a microscope.

Your blood is full of RED BLOOD CELLS that look like little flying saucers. They carry oxygen around your body. These cells have iron in them, from a chemical called haemoglobin, and this makes them look red.

We can also see WHITE BLOOD CELLS and their job is to fight infection. If you cut yourself, these cells rush to the wound and fight any germs there.

The blood will also clot, as otherwise you might not stop bleeding! Little fragments of cells called PLATELETS (because they look like little plates) help to clump together and form a mesh. This also protects the wound.

About half of your blood is made up of PLASMA, which carries all these other types of cells around.

Next time you injure yourself, think of this: in a single drop of your blood, there are 4 million red blood cells, 10,000 white blood cells and 300,000 platelets. That's a bloody lot!

Blood passes along **BLOOD VESSELS** to get all over your body. It flows from the heart through **ARTERIES** to get to your lungs where it picks up the oxygen you breath in.

The **HEART** is the pump that pushes your blood around your body. If you live to be 75, your heart will have beaten 2.5 billion times.

THE HEART OF IT ALL

It then moves all over your body's cells, giving oxygen to your cells, and then goes back to your heart through **VEINS**.

Nutrients and oxygen are passed to your body's cells through small tubes called **CAPILLARIES** that connect arteries and veins.

The biggest heart in nature is in the blue whale. It is as big as a small car and pumps 220 litres of blood with every heartbeat.

THE IMMUNE SYSTEM

When you're feeling awful with a cold or the flu, or when you have a cut that becomes sore, it's likely that **germs** like viruses or bacteria are doing mischief. These invaders can enter our bodies through our lungs if we breathe them in, through our mouths from food that's gone off or through a cut in our skin.

Your immune system keeps you alive in the constant battle against germs that want to eat your lunch — and then you. The first defence system is the SKIN. This acts as a barrier to keep germs from getting into your body. If germs try to enter through your nose or mouth, they have to make it through a layer of slimy wet stuff called MUCOUS (which you probably call bogies).

But if the germs make it past these defences to set up camp in your bloodstream, it's time to call on the big guns.

GETTING EX-CYTED

The main warriors for your immune system are LEUCOCYTES, or white blood cells. They make up an army that defends your body from germs.

MACROPHAGES (which means 'big eater') are a type of leucocyte. They are your guard cells. They have special sensors which detect bacteria or viruses and tell them to start chomping — just like when you sense some chocolate and stuff it in your mouth!

T-Helper Cell

B Cell

Neutrophil

Leucocyte (White Blood Cell)

Macrophage (Big Eater)

BOOM

BUGS

- B CELLS are the weapons factory of the immune system. They make ANTIBODIES, which are like attack dogs — they latch on to bacteria and kill them on contact. Antibodies can also act like a sticky goo, allowing macrophages to get a hold of bacteria and eat them.

If they can't control the infection on their own, they need backup. T HELPER CELLS act as a messenger — they get on their horses and call for reinforcements if a fight breaks out.

NEUTROPHILS are another type of leucocyte that can eat bacteria and kill them, using a powerful chemical a bit like the bleach that's used to clean your toilet!

WANTED
MR HUM BUG

TELLING FRIEND FROM FOE

When you are very young, your immune system is still learning (like you). It hasn't come in contact with many germs, so it might work more slowly. Older people have weaker immune systems because, like other parts of the body, the immune system doesn't work as well as the body gets older. But for most of your life, it works just fine! You can keep your immune system healthy by getting a good night's sleep, eating healthy food and taking regular exercise.

Together, these warriors fight off the infection. But it doesn't stop there – the next time you are invaded, your **MEMORY CELLS** remember how to fight. They stick up WANTED posters and once that cowboy rides into town again, the sheriff and his deputies recognise him and kill him straight away.

VACCINATION NATION

IRISH CONNECTION

ALMROTH WRIGHT

Almroth Wright (1861–1947) was a doctor who was educated in Trinity College Dublin and developed a vaccine against typhoid.

VACCINES use your immune system's memory to protect you from diseases. When you were younger, you would have been vaccinated, which meant you were injected with a weakened form of an infection. It didn't cause the disease, but it gently woke up your immune cells, and they were trained to recognise the enemy like they were in a boot camp. If the enemy invades again, they are ready to do battle.

HERD IMMUNITY means that the more people in a population who are vaccinated the better, as the germs have nowhere to hide. This protects people who can't get vaccinated because they are sick or weak.

Vaccines are very powerful and have saved millions of lives. Polio, a disease caused by a virus, has been almost eliminated, and an even worse disease called smallpox was finally wiped out in 1980.

Baa ... ?

49

THE REPRODUCTIVE SYSTEM

All life reproduces, which means that each living thing can make more of itself. Without this ability, life would come to an end very quickly. And that wouldn't be great, now would it?

Some species have a clever trick: they can reproduce ASEXUALLY, which means the female can produce a baby without a male. Bacteria reproduce this way, as do some sharks, lizards and snakes.

But most species of animal reproduce SEXUALLY, which means they need a male and a female (*see how plants do it on page 31*).

Testes and ovaries also produce messenger chemicals called hormones that help your body develop. In men, this means more muscle tissue, a deeper voice and more body hair. Women develop breasts and grow wider hips.

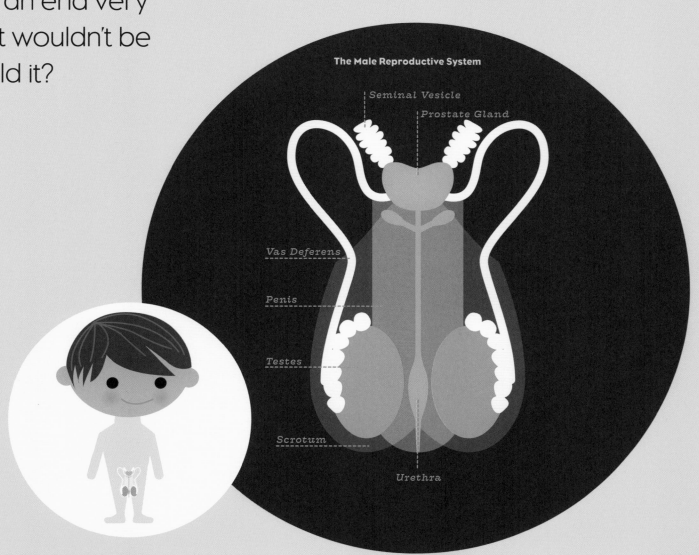

The Male Reproductive System

Seminal Vesicle
Prostate Gland
Vas Deferens
Penis
Testes
Scrotum
Urethra

3

2

1

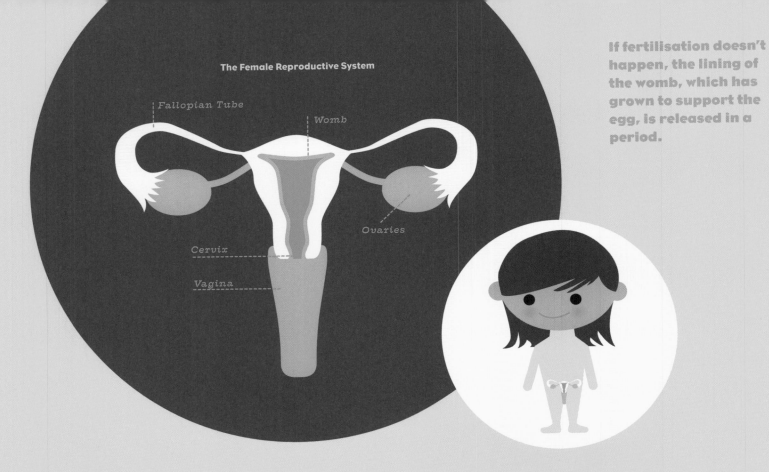

The Female Reproductive System

Fallopian Tube

Womb

Ovaries

Cervix

Vagina

If fertilisation doesn't happen, the lining of the womb, which has grown to support the egg, is released in a period.

In humans, there are two ingredients needed to make a baby: an EGG from the woman and a SPERM from the man.

A woman has two OVARIES, which release an egg each month.

Sperm are made in the TESTES (also called testicles) in a man's body.

During SEX, the sperm move from the testes through a tube and are released from the PENIS into the VAGINA.

Once released into the woman, the sperm swim up into the woman's WOMB.

The egg is then FERTILISED by the sperm, and we now have the recipe to make a human.

The fertilised egg will divide and keep dividing until it forms an EMBRYO.

The embryo will grow into a FOETUS, which will continue to develop.

All going well, after nine months a BABY is born.

Around 233 babies are born in Ireland every day. In the world, around 250 babies are born every minute. Imagine: all that new life, all that crying and all that poo. Welcome!

Sometimes, an egg can be fertilised outside the body, and the egg is then put into the woman's womb. This helps couples who have not been able to have a baby. Since 1978, eight million babies have been born in this way.

What's the furthest you've ever swum? If sperm were human beings, they would have to swim from Ireland to France to make it to the egg!

A woman will release up to 400 eggs in her lifetime. A man will produce up to 1 billion sperm in one go.

CELLS

All these amazing systems in our body are made up of **cells**. A cell is a bit like a tiny Lego block. They can live on their own, like in a creature called an amoeba, but when you put lots of them together, they can make a big structure – you!

In your body, there are at least 300 different types of cell (*see how they were cooked up on page 22*). You are a **COLONY** of lots of different members all living together as one big happy family.

As many as 70 billion cells in your body die each day, out of 37 trillion, so you've got plenty to spare. And don't worry, they are quickly replaced.

ODD JOBS

Each cell type in your body has a role to play in keeping your body running smoothly, from your head down to your toes!

The biggest cell in the human body is the egg in a woman's ovaries. It is 1mm across and it can be seen without a microscope. But most cells are much smaller than that. A type of white blood cell called a lymphocyte is only ten-millionths of a metre across. Some cells are very long, like the neuron in the sciatic nerve, which runs from your spinal cord to your big toe.

The biggest cell in nature is an ostrich's egg, which can weigh up to 1.6kg.

HEART CELLS keep your heart beating.

NEURONS in your brain hold your memories.

STOMACH CELLS help you digest food.

WHITE BLOOD CELLS help you fight infections.

RED BLOOD CELLS carry oxygen around your body.

INGRAINED IN THE MEMBRANE

When we look inside cells using a microscope, we can see all kinds of interesting things.

Plant cells have something extra – a green structure called a chloroplast. This is where photosynthesis happens. Plant cells also have a cell wall for protection and a storage chamber called a vacuole.

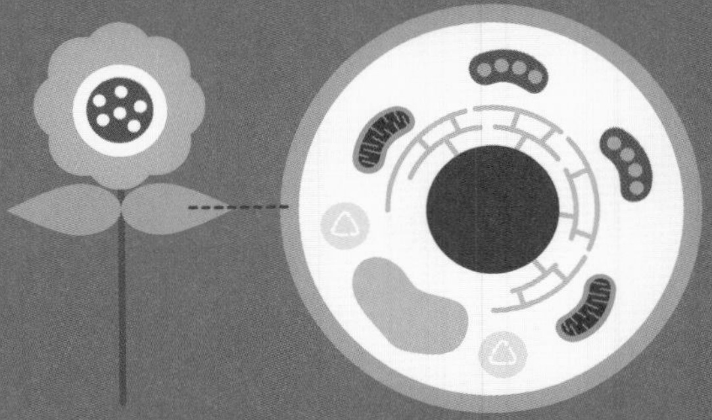

MITOCHONDRIA are where the energy is extracted from the nutrients we eat. They look like grains or threads, and their job is to is to capture energy in something called ATP, which is like a little battery that powers everything in life.

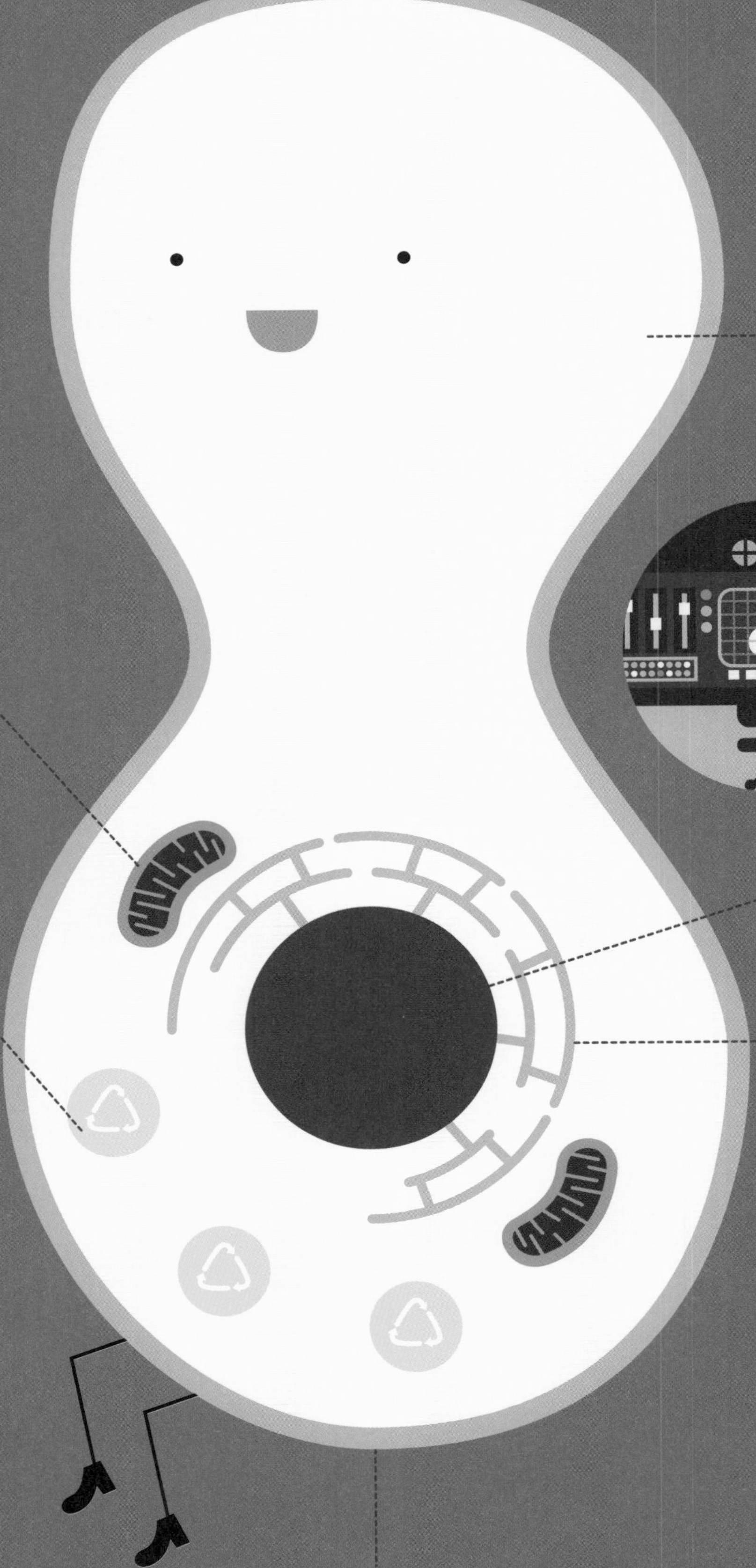

All of these are floating around inside the cell in a gel called the CYTOPLASM.

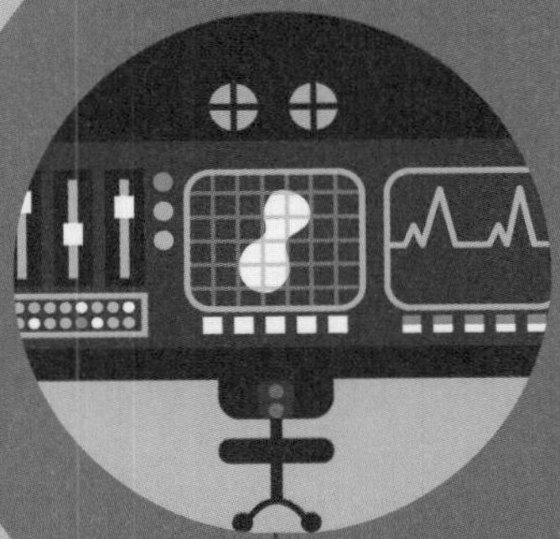

The NUCLEUS is a dark, circular blob and it is the control centre of the cell.

ATP

IRISH CONNECTION

EDWARD CONWAY

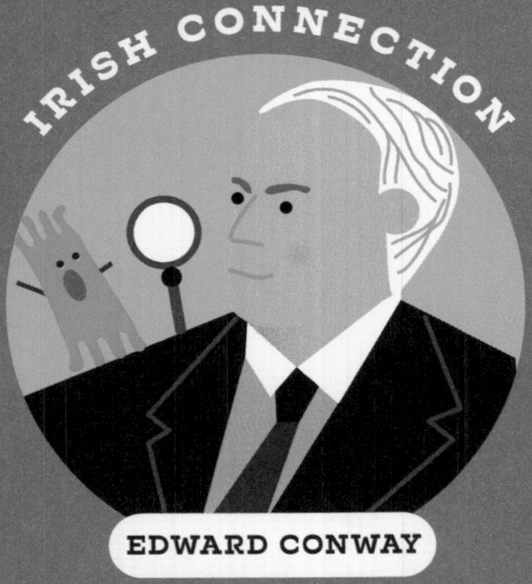

Edward Conway (1894–1968) was a biochemist who was born in Nenagh, County Tipperary. He worked on the chemistry of living tissues, especially muscle and kidneys.

The CELL MEMBRANE holds the cell together.

We can see a long, strung-out thing called the ENDOPLASMIC RETICULUM. This name means 'net inside the cell,' because this is what it looks like under a microscope. It's no ordinary net, though – it's the cell's manufacturing and packaging factory.

GENES

Your eyes might be brown. Your hair might be blonde. People might say you look like your uncle. The reason for these things is that they are written in your **genes**.

Genes in each cell of your body make you what you are. You INHERIT them from your parents – half from your mother and half from your father – and you might eventually pass them on to your children. Genes carry the information that decides your unique features, or TRAITS. The gene from one parent might DOMINATE over the other and so you look more like your mother than your father.

Genes provide the instructions for each cell as it grows and continues to divide. Each cell has around 21,000 genes. Does that seem like a lot to you? Well, humans are a complex engine, and genes are like a big parts list.

Genes are tiny things. You can't see them without a microscope, but they are arranged along what look like tangled strings. These strings are called CHROMOSOMES. You have 23 pairs of chromosomes in each cell – one set comes from your mother, and the other set comes from your father. They are found in the command centre for the cell, the nucleus.

Chromosomes are made of a chemical called DNA. This is one of the most fascinating and famous chemicals ever. DNA stands for deoxyribonucleic acid (*dee-ox-see-rye-boh-new-klay-ick acid*) – but it's easier to just say DNA.

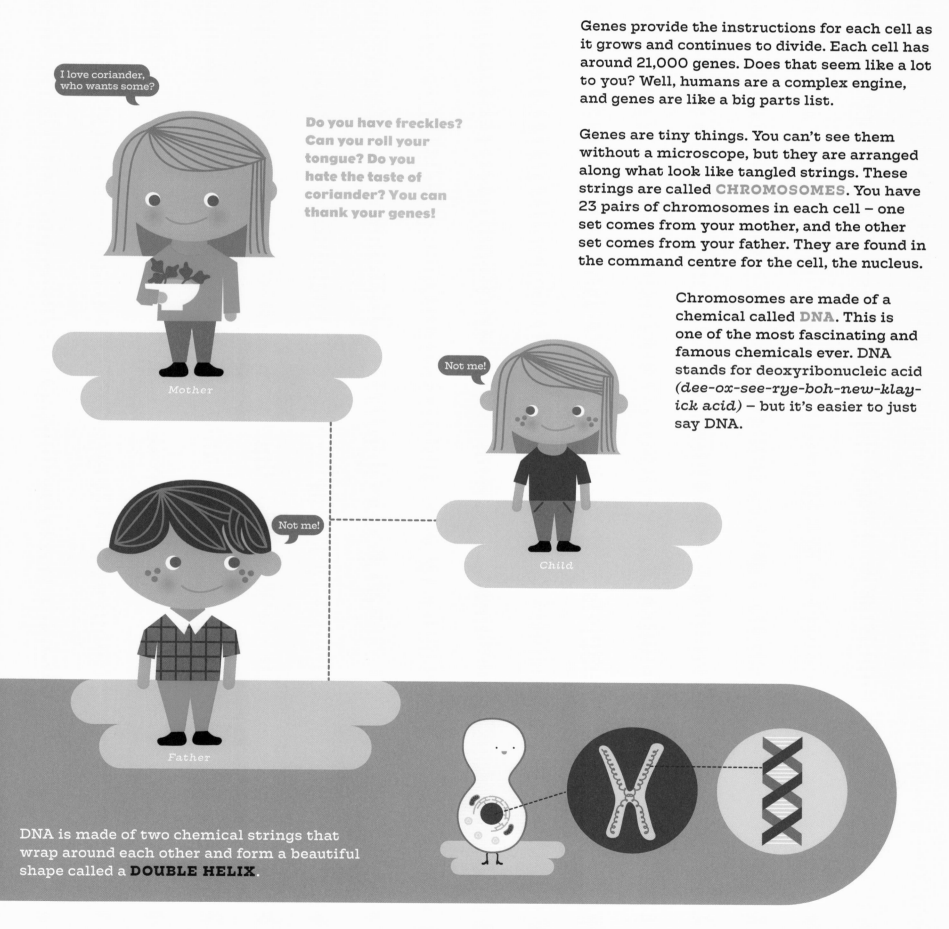

Do you have freckles? Can you roll your tongue? Do you hate the taste of coriander? You can thank your genes!

I love coriander, who wants some?

Mother

Not me!

Child

Not me!

Father

DNA is made of two chemical strings that wrap around each other and form a beautiful shape called a **DOUBLE HELIX**.

Humans share 99% of the same DNA with other humans, 96% with chimpanzees, and 60% with bananas!

When a cell divides, it makes two identical copies of itself. A cell copies its DNA by unravelling the double helix and then copying each of the strings. One copy goes into each of the cells that are made, and hey presto, we have two cells where once there was one. This process is called MITOSIS.

Mitosis is like a house splitting itself in half, separating, and then repairing the walls and plumbing to make two houses!

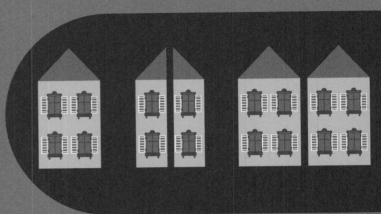

Scientists called GENETICISTS love studying genes because they explain so much about how the body works. They also know that when a gene is broken, this can cause diseases. It might be possible to fix broken genes and stop diseases in their tracks. Wouldn't that be gene-ius?

Now I know why I peel in the sun!

This is bananas!

We are family ...

IRISH CONNECTION

ERWIN SCHRÖDINGER

In 1943, an important event happened in Dublin. A famous physicist called Erwin Schrödinger gave a talk called 'What is Life?'. This inspired other scientists to work on the chemical that makes genes – DNA.

LIFE'S BUILDING BLOCKS

You hear the word **protein** and I'll bet the first thing that crosses your mind is food, right? Well, yes, but proteins go way beyond that. We need protein in our diet to make more proteins in our own bodies, because proteins do everything in biology. Like bodybuilders, proteins do the heavy lifting.

Different proteins do different things. Some are enzymes for digesting food. Some build muscles, bone, hair and skin. Some are important for defending us from infection and some carry oxygen around your body. Others are hormones, messengers released into the blood to send signals.

A typical cell in your body holds as many as 100,000 different types of protein.

Each protein is different, like a necklace that folds up into a particular shape. Each bead on these necklaces is an AMINO ACID. There are 20 of them in total, and they have long names like glycine and tryptophan (now that's a mouthful). Our bodies can make some of them, but we must get the others from our food, so they are called essential amino acids.

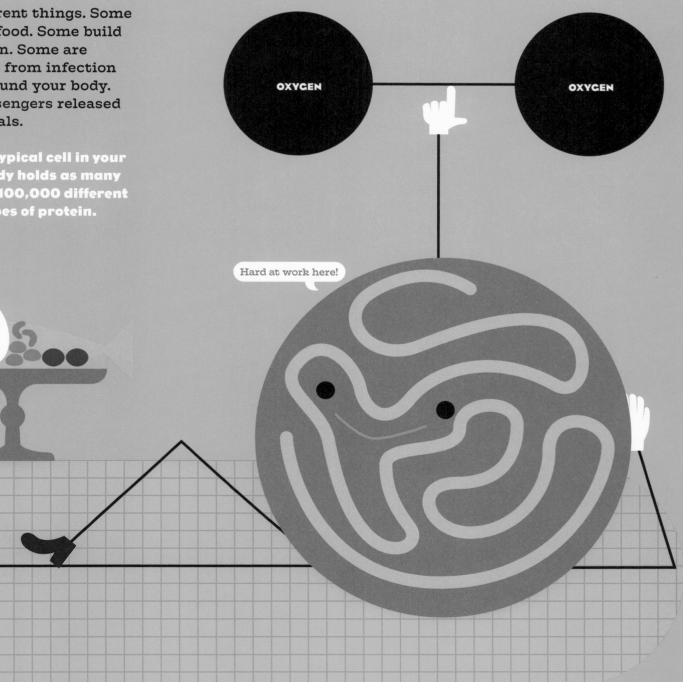

OXYGEN

OXYGEN

Hard at work here!

LOST IN TRANSLATION?

The body makes new proteins in a pretty special way. Each gene is made up of DNA. The information in the DNA is copied by an enzyme to make RNA.

DNA and RNA are quite similar, so this is called TRANSCRIPTION, which is another name for copying something down.

The RNA then brings amino acids together to make a protein. Because protein is very different from RNA, this is called TRANSLATION.

Once the protein is made, it FOLDS into complicated shapes and then goes off to do its job, whatever that might be.

Think of DNA as the English language, and each gene as a different word. Your DNA writes down lots of words with RNA, making up a story. The RNA then translates the story into a different language, like Irish. The story then comes to life in proteins. Bet you didn't know all of life works a bit like your Irish homework!

FRIDGE 2100 ❄❄❄

The other two building blocks for life are CARBOHYDRATES and FATS.

Glucose is an example of a carbohydrate, and our muscles burn a lot of it to provide energy to our cells. That energy will have started in the sun, which plants absorb and use to make sugar. When you eat a sugary food like fruit, your body is capturing the energy that began in sunlight.

FATS are also a very good source of energy. Burning fat in our bodies is a bit like burning oil. We store fat in our bodies for when we need it, but if we overeat we store too much and become overweight.

IRISH CONNECTION

CHARLES McMUNN

Charles McMunn (1852–1911) was from Easkey, County Sligo. He was the first person to describe proteins called cytochromes, which are important in getting energy from nutrients.

THE MICROSCOPIC WORLD

Your body is great. It allows you to do all sorts of things. But sometimes, you might get sick. The word **disease** means that something isn't working properly in a part of your body. Hopefully, you will get better on your own, or with the help of your doctor. Many different medicines can help you, and **biomedical scientists** are always looking for cures or ways to prevent diseases.

Welcome to the microscopic world! Watch out - there are some nasty things down here. INFECTIOUS DISEASES are caused by tiny germs invading your body. When somebody says to wash your hands, they are telling you to wash the microscopic germs off.

Did you know that there are up to 4 million bacteria on every square centimetre of skin on your hands? Always wash with soap and hot water, otherwise you're just giving the germs a bath!

BACTERIA are found everywhere, even in the clouds. They are one-millionth the size of you! Under ideal conditions, they can reproduce very quickly, dividing once every 20 minutes, which means that within 12 hours, a single bacterium will turn into 34 billion — almost five times the population of the Earth! We use helpful bacteria to make cheese and the bacteria in our stomachs help us digest food. Some types are dangerous, though, and cause diseases like tuberculosis, which damages your lungs. Bacteria can be killed by antibiotics, but worryingly, some bacteria are getting better at dodging them.

VIRUSES are much smaller than bacteria, and they can only be seen with very powerful microscopes. Viruses can't live for long on their own. They invade our cells and use them for themselves — a bit like your brother who never buys any food but eats all of yours! Viruses cause diseases like measles, which covers your skin in red blotches. Viral diseases are hard to treat, but vaccines protect us from many of them.

Did you know that antibiotics can't help if you have a virus like a cold or flu?

Giddy up!

PARASITES cause diseases like malaria, which is spread by mosquitoes and affects millions of people.

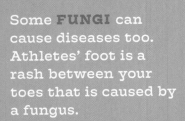

Some **FUNGI** can cause diseases too. Athletes' foot is a rash between your toes that is caused by a fungus.

I'm itching to get rid of my athlete's foot!

An **AUTOIMMUNE** disease is when your immune system attacks your own body and makes you sick. For example, in arthritis, it attacks your joints, and in multiple sclerosis, it attacks your nervous system. We still don't know why.

HEART DISEASE happens when your arteries become clogged with fat, which can stop blood flow to your heart. Drugs that stop your body making a fat called cholesterol, or a healthy diet and exercise can lower the risk of heart disease.

POISON

CANCER is a disease that causes your own cells to change. They keep making copies of themselves, forming something called a tumour. The main treatment is to poison the cancer cells, although a new treatment gets your own immune system to kill them off.

Finally, all life on Earth **AGES**, including you, and we don't really know why. As your body gets older, you'll be less able to do things like you used to. Diseases of the brain like Alzheimer's disease (which affects memory) and Parkinson's disease (which affects movement) become more common.

But eventually, our bodies will stop working, and we will **DIE**. This is part of life, but it can be very hard to lose someone you love. Our bodies will break down into the same building blocks that make up the rest of the universe – the soil, the trees and even the stars.

Diseases, getting older and death are part of life, but with a healthy lifestyle and medicines to help us, we should live to a ripe old age. Look at Jeanne Calment. She was a French woman who holds the current record, living to 122 years. Beat that!

IRISH CONNECTION

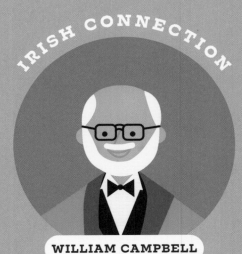

WILLIAM CAMPBELL

William Campbell is an Irish biologist who discovered a treatment for infections caused by parasitic worms, one of which makes people go blind. He was jointly awarded the 2015 Nobel Prize in Physiology or Medicine.

THE HUMAN BODY: THE FUTURE

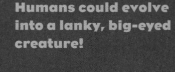

Humans could evolve into a lanky, big-eyed creature!

What will humans be like in 50 years? Well, first of all, you will probably still be around. You might even still be here in 100 years. Modern medicine and better lifestyles have extended the average **lifespan** of humans, and a baby born in Ireland today can expect to live to be one hundred. Get ready for the long haul!

New medicines will continue to be discovered for the diseases that we can't treat now. We might even be able to slow down ageing or replace organs in your body as they wear out.

Way into the future, humans are likely to keep evolving. We might lose our muscles as robots do all the work. If we move to other planets further from the sun, we could develop huge eyes to see better in dim light, and because there's less gravity in space, we might grow longer arms and legs.

But the biggest change that is happening right now is the development of artificial intelligence, or AI. Robots will become more and more sophisticated, and they will carry out many jobs currently being done by humans. Driverless cars, surgical machines and cleaning robots will mean some jobs aren't as necessary any more. Jobs that will survive will involve human contact, like nursing or social work. Artists and scientists will still be needed, as both involve creativity. There will also likely be new jobs that don't exist right now. We've only just begun to get to grips with what artificial intelligence will mean for the humans of the future. But we need to make sure that we use this great science for the benefit of all humanity.

One thing is for sure: your life in 50 years will look nothing like your life now.

BE A
SCIENTIST!

BE AN
ORTHOPAEDIST

Take a clean, dry chicken bone. Without breaking it, try to bend it. See how stiff it is?

Now put the bone in a glass and fill it with vinegar. Leave it for three days.

ORTHOPAEDIST

Take the bone out and dry it. Now try to break it.

The vinegar will have dissolved the calcium in the bone, leaving it weak and flexible. This is why we need calcium in our diet!

BE A
GENETICIST

Put a little water and a pinch of salt in a glass. Now spit in it!

Add some washing-up liquid, grapefruit or pineapple juice, and some drops of ice-cold pure alcohol (a grown-up can get some white spirit from a hardware shop).

GENETICIST

Stir the mixture and you'll notice some white stringy stuff appears.

This is your DNA! It comes from the cells in your saliva. The salt protects the DNA, and the other ingredients break down the proteins around it. The alcohol makes it visible.

BE AN
EXERCISE
PHYSIOLOGIST

Your resting heart rate is a measure of heart health and fitness. At your age, a healthy heart rate is 60 to 100 beats a minute.

To check your resting heart rate, place two fingers on your wrist while you're sitting down.

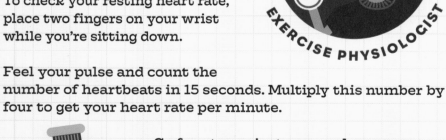
EXERCISE PHYSIOLOGIST

Feel your pulse and count the number of heartbeats in 15 seconds. Multiply this number by four to get your heart rate per minute.

Go for a ten-minute run and measure your pulse again. If it goes up to 90–130 beats per minute you have hit your target heart rate zone, which is good for maintaining fitness.

BE A
BIOCHEMIST

Heat up one cup of milk and add four teaspoons of white vinegar.

Pour the mixture through a strainer and collect the stuff left in the strainer.

BIOCHEMIST

Mould it into a shape and leave it for a day to harden.

A protein in the milk has changed because of the vinegar. You've made plastic milk!

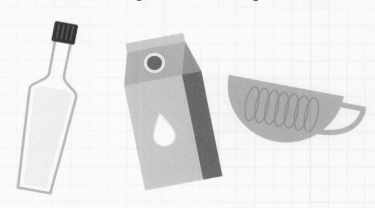

Welcome to my world!

THE VERY SMALL

We last left off with the microscopic world, which is pretty small. But things are about to get a whole lot smaller as we start to take apart the tiny pieces of the universe.

We'll look at matter and chemicals, and we'll see that they are made up of even tinier things, until we get down to the very building blocks of the universe – atoms.

But it doesn't stop there. Atoms are made of even smaller things: protons, neutrons, electrons and beyond.

Down here, in the world of the very small, things work a little strangely. All sorts of phenomenal phenomena like energy and light are bouncing around, and we'll cover everything from gravity to the weird world of relativity.

At the end, we'll get to the very fundamental forces that hold the entire universe together, bringing us right back up from the very small to the impossibly large.

Phew!

MATTER

What is mind? Doesn't matter. What is matter? Never mind! Well, we should mind a little bit. **Matter** is the name that scientists give to everything that you can touch, see, feel or smell around you.

CHEMISTRY is the branch of science that deals with matter. Scientists called chemists keep making new chemicals that help us in all kinds of ways, including new medicines, electronic devices like your smartphone and fertilizers to help crops grow.

A MASSIVE STATE

MASS is a measure of the amount of matter in an object. Your mass is different from your weight, which is actually the force of gravity pulling you towards the Earth. The moon has less gravity, so if you were there, you'd weigh $\frac{1}{6}$ th as much – but your mass would be the same!

Matter is made of tiny pieces called **PARTICLES**. These vibrate, but you can't feel it because they are so small. Depending on how fast the particles are vibrating, matter can be in different **STATES**.

Matter can change state when energy is added or removed. If you heat up a solid, like ice, the energy makes the particles move faster and it will change into a liquid (water). If you keep the heat on, the particles move even faster and it will turn into a gas (water vapour).

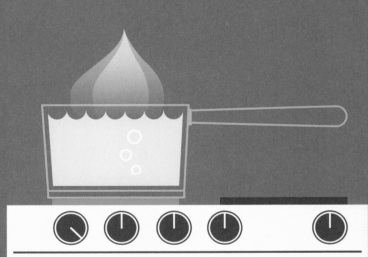

A **SOLID** has a definite shape and volume (which is the space it fills). The particles in a solid are vibrating slowly and are tightly packed together.

A **LIQUID** has a definite volume, but it takes the shape of the container it is in. The particles in a liquid are vibrating faster, but are still close together.

A **GAS** spreads out to fill the entire volume of a container. Gases vibrate the fastest, and their particles are further apart – but they can be put under pressure and compressed.

Solid

Liquid

Gas

SO BASIC

Chemists are also interested in whether matter is **ACIDIC** or **BASIC**. We measure this using a scale called **pH** – the lower the pH, the more acidic the matter is. Lemon juice has a pH of 2, while soapy water has a pH of 12. We use acids and bases for all kinds of things from cleaning to cooking. Baking soda is a base that helps bread dough to rise. Sulphuric acid is one of the most dangerous chemicals in the world, and has been used by criminals to destroy evidence ...

Better be careful!

SOAP

Both acids and bases can hurt you. Bee stings are acidic while lye, a base found in soap, can burn you. Ouch!

Our baking has just risen to new levels.

IRISH CONNECTION

I'm like a diamond, I work best under pressure.

ROBERT BOYLE

BAKERY

BAKING SODA

At least you'll make a lot of dough!

Robert Boyle (1627–1691) was born in County Waterford, and he was the first modern chemist. He came up with Boyle's Law, which describes the relationship between the pressure and volume of a gas.

ATOMS

All matter is made of tiny building blocks called **atoms**. These are so small that it takes billions and billions of them to make something you can see. Only our most powerful microscopes allow us to see individual atoms. A drop of water has two sextillion atoms of oxygen. A sheet of paper is almost half a million atoms thick!

Don't trust atoms – they make up everything ...

Computer company IBM made a miniature movie by moving atoms around! 'A Boy and his Atom' holds the Guinness World Record for the world's smallest film.

Pass the popcorn, please.

UP AND ATOM

Let's have a look at an atom. The NUCLEUS is at the centre of the atom, and it is made of particles called PROTONS and NEUTRONS.

Other particles called ELECTRONS orbit the nucleus at incredible speeds. They are much smaller than protons and they move so fast that physicists are never sure of their exact position. They're here and suddenly they're there – you can never pin them down.

These three particles have difference electrical CHARGES. Protons carry a positive charge, electrons are negative, and the neutron has no charge – it's neutral! Atoms usually have the same number of electrons and protons – the negative charges balance out the positive charges.

When you touch something made up of atoms, like your table, it feels solid. But atoms are 99.99% empty space!

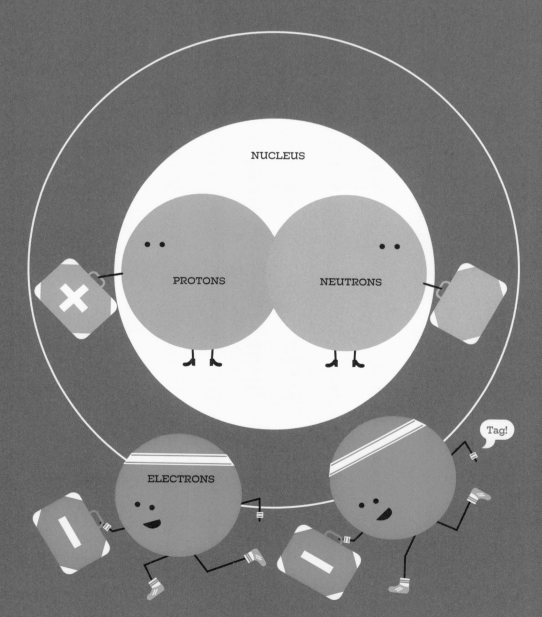

NUCLEUS

PROTONS   NEUTRONS

ELECTRONS

Tag!

I'm positive!   I'm neutral.   I'm negative ...

QUARKY STUFF

Then there are even smaller particles in each atom. Neutrons and protons are made of particles called QUARKS. This word is from a novel called *Finnegans Wake* by the famous Irish writer James Joyce. It gets even stranger, because these quarks have different 'flavours', like strange, bottom and charmed. I wonder if there's a chocolate flavour?

We'd better stop there – things are getting a bit silly! And how do we even know these tiny particles are there? Well, physicists have smashed them together to break them up and find out what's inside. Think of it like smashing a chocolate egg full of Smarties into an egg filled with M&M's. Maybe they'll find a chocolate-flavoured quark after all ...

Atom smashing is done in machines called PARTICLE ACCELERATORS. The world's largest accelerator is the Large Hadron Collider at CERN in Geneva. It is a 27km-long underground tunnel in the shape of a circle. It is the biggest and most expensive single machine ever built, costing $13 billion to build, and over 10,000 scientists are working on it (see what they're looking for on page 9).

In 2012, after years of atom smashing, scientists reported the discovery of the Higgs Boson. The Higgs Boson is thought to explain how other particles get their mass – without it, nothing would exist.

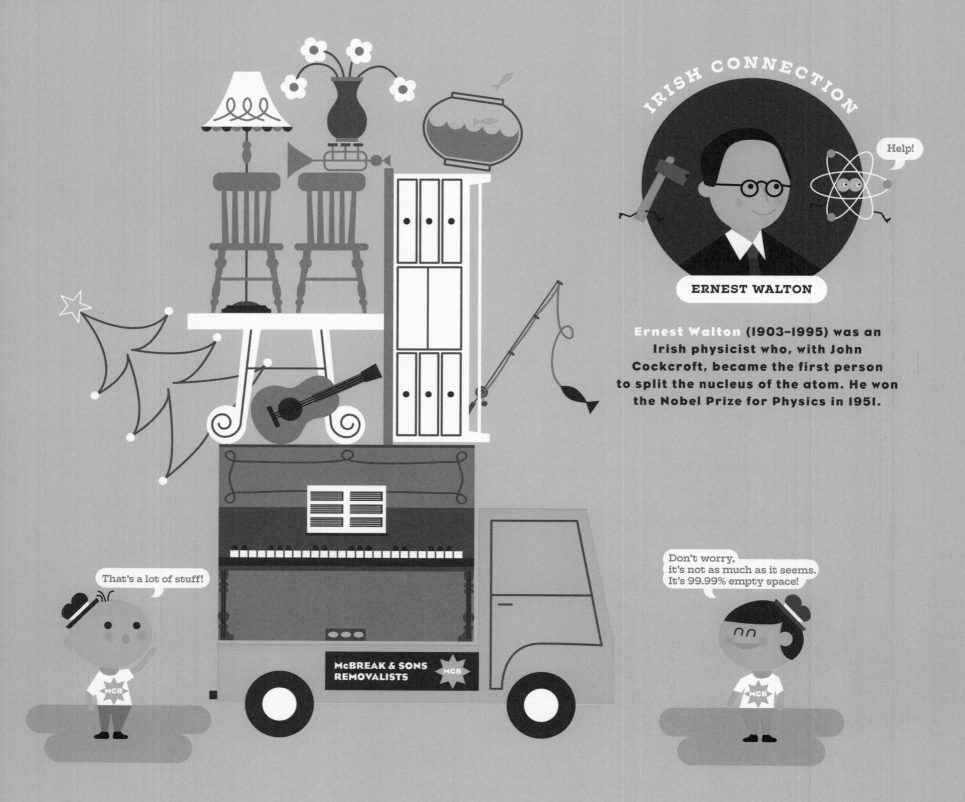

That's a lot of stuff!

McBREAK & SONS REMOVALISTS

Don't worry, it's not as much as it seems. It's 99.99% empty space!

IRISH CONNECTION

Help!

ERNEST WALTON

Ernest Walton (1903–1995) was an Irish physicist who, with John Cockcroft, became the first person to split the nucleus of the atom. He won the Nobel Prize for Physics in 1951.

ELEMENTS

An **element** is something that can't be chemically broken down into something else. Everything in the universe is made of these ingredients – you, the planets, and even your teacher.

Hydrogen and helium are the most common elements in the universe. In the Earth's crust, oxygen and silicon are the most common, followed by aluminium and iron.

State of Matter
Solid
Liquid
Gas

ELEMENTARY, MY DEAR

In ancient times, people used to believe that there were only four elements – earth, water, air and fire. We've found a few more since then! Today, scientists have discovered 118 elements altogether and each one has its own name and symbol.

Some are easy: H is for hydrogen. Some are a bit more complex, like lead (Pb). In ancient times, lead was used to make water pipes. The Latin word for waterworks is *plumbum*, so they used Pb as the element's symbol. (This is also where the word plumber comes from – not because they have purple bums!)

Irish chemist Adair Crawford discovered an element in the mines near the Scottish town of Strontian. The element was later called strontium. It's the only element with Irish words, because the name is from the Scots Gaelic 'Sròn an t-Sìthein', which means 'nose of the fairy hill'. Maybe the fairies knew about the magic of strontium – it gives fireworks a brilliant red colour.

All the elements are very different. Many are metals, some are gases, some are hard, some are soft. It was tricky to keep track of all these different types, but in 1869, Russian chemist Dmitri Mendeleev came up with a system for organising them – the **PERIODIC TABLE**.

Each element has its own type of atom. Atoms have different numbers of protons, neutrons and electrons. In the Periodic Table, the elements are listed in the order of the number of protons they have. The number of protons is the **ATOMIC NUMBER** of the element. For example, helium has an atomic number of two, because it has two protons and two neutrons in its nucleus, and two electrons orbiting around it.

We call each column a **GROUP**, and there are 18 groups in total. Each element in a group will have similar **PROPERTIES**, like the temperatures they boil or melt at, or how dense they are.

IRISH CONNECTION

KATHLEEN LONSDALE

Dame Kathleen Lonsdale (1903–1971) was born in Newbridge, County Kildare. She made a huge contribution to chemistry by working out the shape of chemicals like benzene.

92

URANIUM HEAVY

At last, I got to be the lead character!

← Plumbum

82

CHEMICAL BROTHERS

Some elements can exist on their own, like **GOLD**. Others bond together to form a **MOLECULE**. The gas **OXYGEN** is a molecule with two oxygen atoms. That's why its chemical symbol is O_2.

Oxygen (O)   +   Oxygen (O)   =   Oxygen (O_2)

If the two atoms are from different elements, they form a **COMPOUND**. (All compounds are molecules, but all molecules are not compounds. Make sense?!). Salt is a compound made up of sodium (Na) and chlorine (Cl), so its chemical symbol is NaCl.

Sodium (Na)   +   Chlorine (Cl)   =   Salt (NaCl)

Chemists spend a lot of time getting compounds to **REACT**. This is when two or more substances change to form a new compound. An example is iron reacting with oxygen – this forms rust. A type of chemical called a **CATALYST** will speed up these reactions.

Did you know that your school is full of the chemical dihydrogen monoxide? Sounds dangerous, maybe you should tell your teacher!

... Well, actually, that's just water! Water is made of two hydrogen atoms joined to one oxygen atom – H_2O. 'Di' means two, and 'mono' means one.

H_2O

ELECTRICITY

Can you feel the electricity in the air? I'm positive I can! Electricity is used to power many things in the world around us. But how does it work?

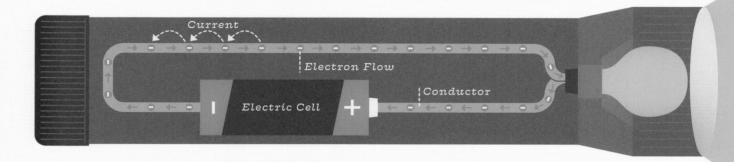

Current · Electron Flow · Electric Cell · Conductor

THE ELECTRIC AVENUE

Atoms usually have the same number of protons and electrons (*get a reminder on page 66*). But when the balance between protons and electrons is changed, an atom can gain or lose an electron. Something has a **POSITIVE CHARGE** if it has more protons than electrons, and a **NEGATIVE CHARGE** if it contains more electrons than protons.

But the universe loves balance, so the extra electrons will travel from one atom to another to try to become neutral again. This movement can be captured and used to power things – and that's **ELECTRICITY**.

When you turn on a torch, electricity is released from the battery in a **CURRENT**. It flows through the wires and is **CONVERTED** by the bulb into the light we see. This makes up a **CIRCUIT**.

A lightning strike is a flow of electrons moving from a cloud to the ground.

FUELLING UP

The electricity that allows you to charge things like your smartphone mainly comes from **FOSSIL FUELS**. But these are causing big problems (*check page 34 for a reminder*), so we need to look at **RENEWABLE ENERGY** – fuels that don't get used up, like the wind, sun and water.

In Ireland, 70% of our electricity comes from coal, gas and oil. We must do better than this!

Countries like Iceland get most of their energy from geothermal sources. If you ever visit, you'll notice a horrible smell, because of gases like hydrogen sulphide. Maybe you should try and capture the energy when you fart!

SOLAR ENERGY captures the energy from the sun in solar panels.

WIND ENERGY is made by huge wind turbines that turn in the wind.

HYDROELECTRIC ENERGY is generated by flowing water that is usually captured in dams.

GEOTHERMAL ENERGY comes from the heat of the Earth.

ELECTRONICS powers the technology we use every day. It can carry the sound of our voice around the world, bring aeroplanes in to land, process huge amounts of information and allow us to access all human knowledge in the palm of our hand.

Electronics works just like electricity, except the current is much tinier, made up of single electrons. We can see the difference in a microwave oven – electricity powers the high-energy waves that cook your food, while electronics controls the timing and the heat level.

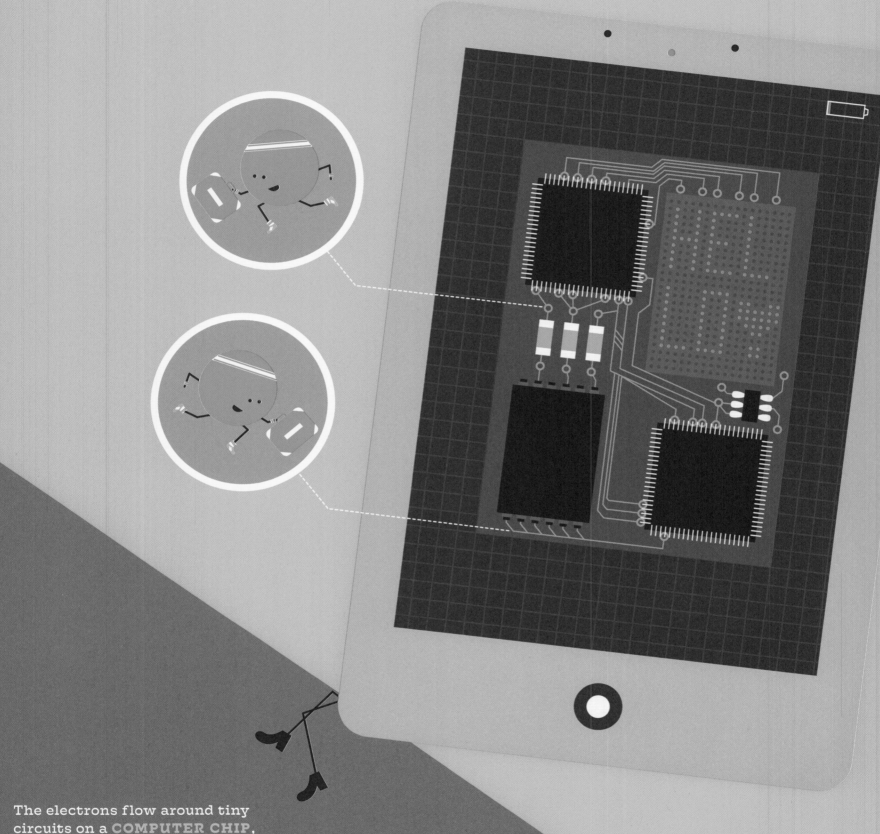

The electrons flow around tiny circuits on a **COMPUTER CHIP**, usually made of silicon. These chips contain millions of electronic components called **TRANSISTORS**.

Computers have many chips on **PRINTED CIRCUIT BOARDS**. Circuit boards have got smaller and smaller – which means smaller electronic devices, like a computer the size of a grain of salt!

In 1965, a computer scientist at Intel came up with Moore's Law, which suggests that the number of transistors in a chip doubles every two years. This might be slowing down. Those computer guys need to try harder!

MAGNETISM

Ancient civilisations like the Greeks, the Romans and the Chinese knew all about **magnets**. They knew they could attract metal, which must have seemed magical. But to be fair, we ourselves still think that any advanced technology seems magical. But at least we understand magnets now!

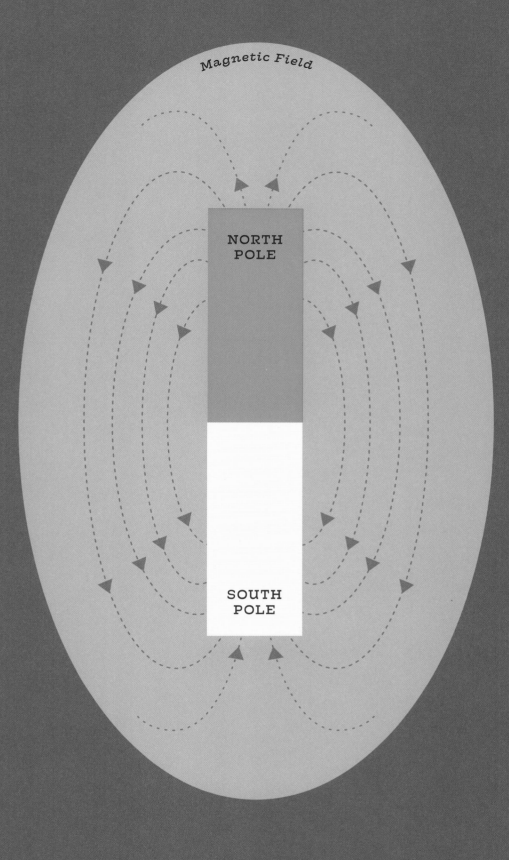

Magnetic Field

NORTH POLE

SOUTH POLE

Excuse me, what direction is east? Or does it go all the way south from here?

Some animals can detect the Earth's magnetic field and use it to guide themselves. Bees, birds, turtles and sharks all find their way around using a built-in magnet in their brains.

A magnet has two ends called POLES. One is called the north pole and the other is called the south pole. The north pole of one magnet REPELS the other magnet's north pole. The north pole of one magnet ATTRACTS the south pole of another magnet. Opposites really do attract!

The poles create an invisible area of force called a MAGNETIC FIELD. A magnetic field can travel through all kinds of things – when you stick a piece of paper to your fridge with a magnet, the field is travelling through the paper.

FINDING OUR WAY

The north pole of a magnet points roughly toward Earth's geographic north pole and the south to the south. This is because the molten rocks and iron in the Earth's core give it a magnetic field of its own – the whole planet acts like a big magnet!

The Earth's magnetic field extends into space, which is known as the MAGNETOSPHERE. When electrons from the sun hit the magnetosphere, the particles become excited and give off the wonderful colours we see as AURORAS – the Northern and Southern Lights.

Some materials are naturally magnetic, like LODESTONE. Others can be temporarily given a magnetic field by the flow of an electric current. The movement of electrons creates a magnetic field in a process called ELECTROMAGNETISM.

One use of electromagnetism is the ELECTRIC MOTOR. Electricity is passed through the motor, which creates a magnetic field. The magnetic field then causes the motor to spin, allowing it to power ... well, just about anything!

Another use of electromagnetism is INDUCTION, which is when movement is used to create electricity. When a wire is moved through a magnetic field, an electric current begins to flow through it. Induction coils are used in power stations to create electricity.

Electromagnets are used in scrapyards to move things around. A large iron disc is connected to a crane, and the disc is moved into place. When the machine's motor is turned on, the disc becomes magnetised, and the crane can pick up heavy pieces of metal.

IRISH CONNECTION

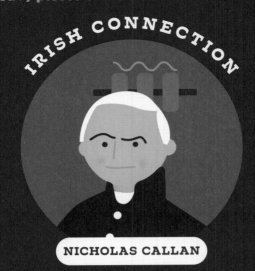

NICHOLAS CALLAN

Nicholas Callan (1799–1864) was a physicist from County Louth who invented the induction coil, which is still on display at the National Science Museum, Maynooth.

ATTRACTIVE USES

A COMPASS contains a magnetic metal needle that points to the north.

MAGNETS are used to write digital information to computers.

MAGLEV (magnetic levitation) railways use magnetism to lift trains off tracks and float them forward or back.

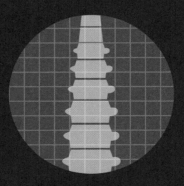

Doctors use a machine called a MAGNETIC RESONANCE IMAGER (MRI) SCANNER to see inside the body.

HEADPHONES use electromagnets to cause vibrations and produce sound.

FORCE AND MOTION

Motion ⟶

The world is full of moving things. Cars whizz by, planes fly overhead and blood rushes around your body. You can ride your bike at top speed (but make sure you wear your helmet). All these things moving from one place to another are in **motion**.

Physicists use the word **WORK** to describe what happens when a force acts on an object to make it move. This might explain why they are sometimes lazy. When they are asked to do normal work, they pretend they don't understand what it is!

MAY THE FORCE BE WITH YOU

Force

Things that are moving can speed up or slow down. The scientific name for the thing that changes this motion is a **FORCE**. (Maybe that's why the Jedi are so pushy.)

Forces can directly move things, like your feet pushing the pedals on your bike. Forces can also stop things from moving – when you stop pedalling, **FRICTION** makes sure you won't roll on for ever. Other forces don't involve things touching – if you go over a ramp, the force of **GRAVITY** will bring you back down to Earth!

Gravity

LIFE IN THE FAST LANE

A force can make something go faster and faster. This is called **ACCELERATION**, and it is calculated by finding out how much distance the object travels every second. The force of Earth's gravity causes an acceleration of 9.8 m/s^2, which means if you drop something from a height, its speed will increase by 9.8 metres per second for each passing second.

A car called the Thrust SSC holds the current land speed record, set in the Black Rock Desert in Nevada. It raced along at 1,223 kilometres per hour, breaking the speed of sound and leaving marks on the sand where the shockwaves hit.

The record for the fastest machine ever built goes to a probe that NASA sent on a mission to the sun. It reached speeds of 253,000 kilometres per hour. Even though it was travelling at an unimaginable speed, it was still only travelling at 0.000234 times the speed of light!

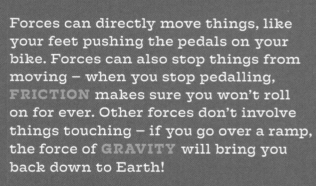

Friction

Acceleration

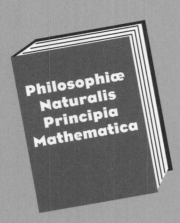

Philosophiæ Naturalis Principia Mathematica

Force

ISAAC'S IDEAS

In 1687, Isaac Newton wrote a book called *Philosophiæ Naturalis Principia Mathematica* (try saying that three times fast!). In it, he described three laws that help us understand how things move (*physicists love laws – see why on page 82*).

The **FIRST LAW** of motion says that any object in motion will continue to move in the same direction, at the same speed, unless a force acts on it. A moving football won't change direction unless you kick or head it away!

The **SECOND LAW** says that the more mass an object has, the more force is needed to make it accelerate. It's easier to score a goal with a football than a bowling ball!

IRISH CONNECTION

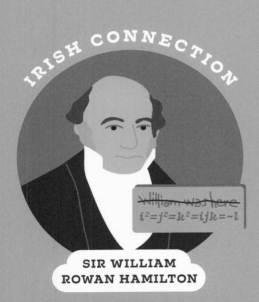

William was here

$i^2 = j^2 = k^2 = ijk = -1$

SIR WILLIAM ROWAN HAMILTON

Sir William Rowan Hamilton (1805– 1865) was from Dublin and is Ireland's most famous mathematician. His equations are used today in space travel and computer games. In 1843, Hamilton carved one of his famous equations on Broome Bridge in Dublin!

Force ---->   <---- Force

The **THIRD LAW** of motion says that whenever a force acts in one direction, it creates an equal force in the opposite direction. When you head the ball, the ball pushes back at you with the same force. Otherwise, the ball would sink into your head and it wouldn't go anywhere. You would lose the football match and be dropped from the team ...

But not to worry – you could become a full-time physicist!

WAVES

I bet you love jumping over waves in the sea or maybe even riding them on a bodyboard. In physics, though, we think about waves a bit differently. A **wave** is a disturbance that travels through space or matter, transferring energy as it goes.

A wave transfers energy, not matter. A Mexican wave can travel around a football stadium without the fans moving position. The people move up and down, and the disturbance is what travels.

ON THE SAME WAVELENGTH

Waves have high points called CRESTS, and low points called TROUGHS.

The WAVELENGTH of a wave is the distance from one crest to the next.

The loudness of the sound depends on the AMPLITUDE.

The pitch of a sound (how high or low it is) depends on the FREQUENCY of the wave.

Wavelength

Crest

Amplitude

What do you mean, 'no surfing'?

Trough

**What do we want?
The Doppler Effect!
When do we want it?....
nooaaAAAwww**

The DOPPLER EFFECT is an apparent change in the frequency and wavelength of a wave. It is caused by the movement of the thing creating the wave and whatever is measuring the wave. Sound complicated?

Well, you've heard it before. Think about a fire engine. As it gets closer to you, the pitch of the siren gets higher and faster – the sound waves are getting bunched up. As it passes by, the pitch gets lower and slower – the waves are spreading out.

Low Frequency

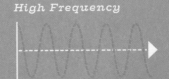
High Frequency

MAKING WAVES

SOUND is a type of mechanical wave that moves through matter and causes our eardrums to vibrate. This vibration is detected in our brains as sound.

In space, no one can hear you scream ... because there's no matter in space, sound can't travel through it.

Sound travels fastest through solids, slower through liquids and slowest through gases. Sound travels about four times faster in water than it does in air. This is why whales can communicate over huge distances in the oceans.

When a jet aircraft reaches the speed of sound, it creates a sonic boom, which is caused by shock waves rippling from the aircraft.

MECHANICAL WAVES have to travel through some kind of matter called a **MEDIUM**. They travel when molecules in the matter bang into each other and pass on the energy.

Eardrum

The second type of wave is called an **ELECTROMAGNETIC WAVE.** It doesn't need a medium, because it is vibrations of electrical and magnetic fields.

Electromagnetic waves fall along a **SPECTRUM**, depending on their wavelength. Radio waves have the longest wavelength – they can be 10 kilometres long! X-rays have a much shorter wavelength at just billionths of a metre.

Most electromagnetic waves are invisible to us (*get a bright idea on page 80*), but special instruments can detect them. Many objects in space give out radio waves. That hissing on your smartphone might be coming from a star, so tune in and you might hear some alien music ...

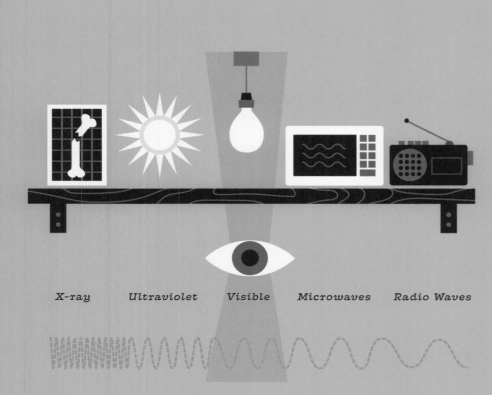

| X-ray | Ultraviolet | Visible | Microwaves | Radio Waves |

IRISH CONNECTION

HELEN MEGAW

Helen Megaw (1907–2002) was a chemist from Dublin who used X-rays to examine different types of crystals. She figured out the structure of ice, and there's an island in Antarctica named after her!

77

ENERGY

When you hear the word energy you might think about running long distances, a power plant generating electricity, or even the sun. It's true that all of these involve energy, but energy can come in lots of different forms. Let's have a look at some of them.

One of the rules of the universe is that energy is never created or destroyed; it just changes its form. You're very good at transforming chemical energy into kinetic energy – just by eating your lunch and running around!

Energy

A BUNDLE OF ENERGY

All moving things have **KINETIC ENERGY**. The flow of water and the wind are examples.

POTENTIAL ENERGY is energy that's stored because of an object's position. A stretched elastic band has lots of potential energy. Watch out!

CHEMICAL ENERGY is the energy in chemicals which can be used to power other things. Petrol has a lot of chemical energy and is used to make engines work.

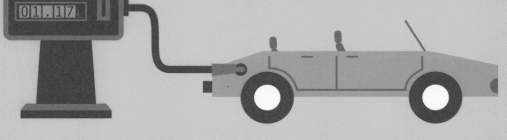

NUCLEAR ENERGY is released when atoms either fuse together or break apart. It can be used to make electricity in nuclear power stations – or to make huge bombs.

HEAT ENERGY Heat energy is caused by matter moving: the faster it moves, the hotter it gets. Temperature is a measure of how fast the tiny pieces of matter are moving. How heat and energy work together is called thermodynamics and it is a very important branch of physics.

ORDER IN THE ENERGY COURT

There are three laws that help us understand how energy works (science has more rules than GAA!).

1 The **FIRST LAW** states that the total amount of energy in a closed system like the universe is always the same. Remember, energy can't be created or destroyed — it just changes from one type into another.

Scientists have tried for centuries to make a perpetual motion machine – a machine that can do work for ever without an energy source. It's impossible, because it would break the first and second laws. Still, you never know, maybe you could think of one!

2 The **SECOND LAW** states that disorder (which means things moving randomly) always increases. You can use this one as an excuse never to tidy your room. Tidying is trying to defy the second law of thermodynamics — tell that to your parents!

Hopefully your parents aren't physicists, because they'd know that disorder can sometimes decrease if order increases elsewhere - they might use this fact to make you tidy the whole house.

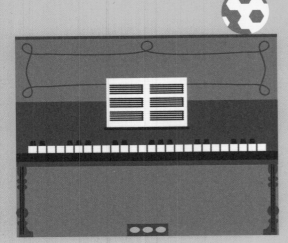

Yum, yum.

3 The **THIRD LAW** tells us that all particles stop moving at a temperature called **ABSOLUTE ZERO**, or 0 Kelvin (−273°C). This is very, very, *very* cold, so cold that molecules can't move at all. You can't get colder than this.

It's impossible to cool something to absolute zero, because the matter around it would warm it up. The only way would be to take it out of our universe!

Wow, that's really cool!

-273

MIGRATION OFFICE

LIGHT

To a scientist, **light** is a fascination. It travels at the remarkable speed of 300,000 kilometres per second. This is the fastest thing in the universe. It's the fastest that anything *can* go in the universe – the cosmic speed limit.

What was that?

Hi and goodbye!

ANY RAY...

But what is light? Light is a form of energy that travels in straight lines called **RAYS** from the sun. It is part of the electromagnetic spectrum (*wave to page 77*). Once it hits off a mirror, it bounces back, because it is moving in a **WAVE**.

Sounds simple? Not so fast. Light can also behave like a **PARTICLE**. A beam of light is made of billions of these particles, all travelling in the same direction. Light has what physicists call **WAVE–PARTICLE DUALITY** – it can be both at the same time. Argh!

Light is made up of tiny packets called photons. A photon is smaller than an atom, so small it doesn't even have a real size. The smallest particle of anything is called a quantum. We're down in the world of quantum mechanics now, dealing with tiny pieces of the universe. (If you add the word quantum to anything, it will sound much more impressive. Like quantum beekeeping.)

What do you mean 'real size'? I'm right here!

HOW EXCITING!

It seems simple, but the way light travels is a pretty impressive trick.

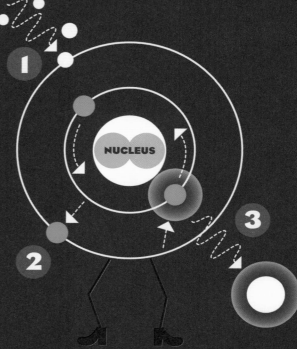

1. Light rays made of photons come from a **SOURCE**, like the sun, and bang into atoms in their path.

2. The atoms become **EXCITED**. This makes the electrons jump to a higher energy level.

NUCLEUS

3. But the electron is **UNSTABLE** up there, so it falls back down, releasing the extra energy as more photons.

And all this happens too fast for us to see!

Refraction

White Light

Prism

SEE THE LIGHT

One of the most unusual things about light is COLOUR. White light is made up of a SPECTRUM of many colours all mixed together.

Isaac Newton named seven — red, orange, yellow, green, blue, indigo and violet. When you see a yellow flower, the yellow light is bouncing off the flower, and the other colours are being absorbed. Blue light bounces off the air more than other colours, and so we see the sky as blue.

LENSES are pieces of curved see-through material that bend light in a process called REFRACTION.

Glass lenses can be used to focus, magnify or bring things that are far away closer. The invention of lenses allowed humans to develop telescopes and microscopes.

Light can be separated, or DISPERSED, by shining it through a special shape called a prism. Some prisms are natural, like raindrops. When light shines through the tiny drops, the colours separate, and we see the light as a RAINBOW.

LASERS are highly focused light, and they are used in science, medicine and construction (and sometimes to distract cats). Another use is in FIBRE-OPTICS, where electrical signals from your computer are converted into lasers and travel down the cable to another computer. Without light, there would be no internet - so shine on!

A photon walks into a hotel. The manager says, 'Welcome to our hotel. Can we help with your luggage?' The photon says, 'No thanks, I'm traveling light!'

IRISH CONNECTION

JOHN TYNDALL

John Tyndall (1820–1893) was born in County Carlow. He worked on magnetism and greenhouse gases but is most famous for explaining why the sky is blue.

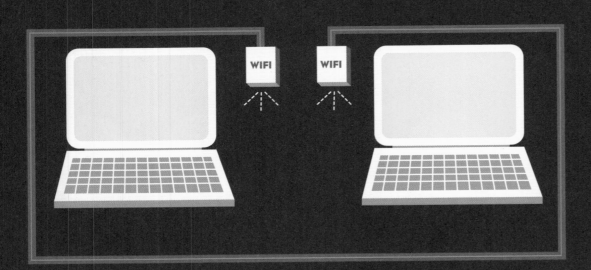

WIFI WIFI

FUNDAMENTAL FORCES

One of the goals of science is to be able to predict things. If you drop a stone, you can predict that it will fall to the ground because of gravity. This is always true. A dropped stone never jumps up (or at least if it did, you'd get a terrible surprise).

FORCE 1

LAWFUL LIVING

What all of this means is the universe has LAWS. They're called laws because they must be followed, but the difference with a scientific law is that it can't be broken. These laws allow us to understand everything from electrons to whole galaxies.

For example, Isaac Newton came up with the LAW OF GRAVITATION, which says that two objects, whatever their mass, will be attracted to one another by the force of gravity. Newton supposedly came up with this law when an apple fell on his head. I wonder if he ate it? (*More apples on page 43.*)

Albert Einstein refined Newton's ideas about gravity. He saw it as a bend in space caused by mass, like a bowling ball on a rubber sheet. He became famous for his equation $E = mc^2$. This describes the relationship between energy (E), mass (m) and the speed of light (c). This is the most famous equation of them all – you'll see it on lots of T-shirts!

A FUN-DAMENTAL FEELING

Gravity sounds like a pretty strong force, right? You can feel it as weight when you try to pick something up. Well, it should be – it's one of the FOUR FUNDAMENTAL FORCES that hold our universe together. But it's actually the weakest of the four!

I was inside and didn't notice the fall! Even though the apple fell, I was not moving inside the apple.

Einstein's theory of relativity explains two weird things about our universe.

As things speed up, time slows down. Imagine that two really accurate clocks are set with the same time and one is sent into space in a fast rocket and brought back to Earth. Time will have passed more slowly on the fast-moving clock, so it will show an earlier time than the clock that didn't move.

The second weird thing is that as things move, they contract. A ruler will shrink as it moves through space, and it will expand again as it slows down. Freaky!

MOON & BACK STANDARD

LAUNCH

DEPARTURE TIME   ARRIVAL TIME

XS2050 CONTROL PANEL

MOON & BACK EXPRESS

LAUNCH

DEPARTURE TIME   ARRIVAL TIME

XP2500 CONTROL PANEL

The second is **ELECTROMAGNETISM** *(recharge on page 73)*. Electricity, magnetism and light are all produced by this interaction. You can see gravity and electromagnetism in action in everyday life, but the last two interactions work down on the tiny level of atoms.

FORCE 2

FORCE 3

The third is the **WEAK NUCLEAR FORCE**. While the other forces hold atoms together, the weak force plays a greater role in things falling apart, or **DECAYING**. This happens when a neutron in the nucleus changes into a proton and an electron. This is then pushed out from the nucleus in a form of energy called **RADIATION**.

I wish I was an electron or a proton ... I would be so radiant!

NEUTRON

PROTON

Radiation

Radiation can harm people and cause cancer. But it can also be useful in medicine and for generating power. The problem with nuclear power plants is the radioactive waste they create. This must be stored in concrete bunkers for a very long time before it becomes safe.

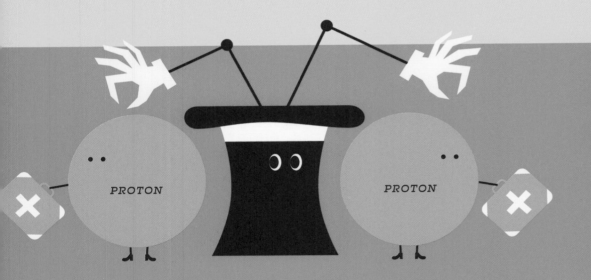

PROTON

PROTON

HOLDING IT TOGETHER

With these fundamental forces, we have finally reached a scale so small it's completely invisible. And yet we know they are there. Without them you — and all matter everywhere — would fall apart into nothingness.

But there's a fourth, even stronger force — and it's the strongest in the universe. We know from electromagnetism that opposites attract, and like repels *(get a reminder on page 72)*. We also know that the nucleus of atoms is full of positively charged protons — so they should be flying away from each other. But they're not. *Something* is keeping these protons side by side, even though they have the same charge. We call this the **STRONG NUCLEAR FORCE**, and, well ... it keeps all the matter in the universe together.

FORCE 4

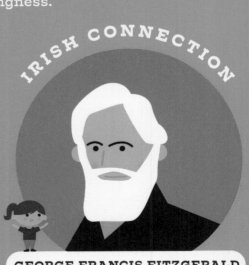

IRISH CONNECTION

GEORGE FRANCIS FITZGERALD

George Francis Fitzgerald (1851–1901) was born in Dublin. He was a physicist who described how moving objects become shorter, and his work was later used by Einstein.

THE VERY SMALL: THE FUTURE

Very exciting things are happening in the world of the very small.

Chemists are always working hard: making brand new medicines to use against diseases; helping to capture energy from renewable sources; and improving batteries for cars and other machines. They're making cool new things like nano-sponge chargers that will charge your phone in your pocket, artificial retinas to enhance your vision, and clothes that give out light. There's an awful lot more chemistry to be done and it will touch every aspect of our lives.

Meanwhile, the atom-busting Large Hadron Collider is cranking up for another proton-bashing session. It's already produced 300 million gigabytes of data, the same amount as streaming videos for 1,000 years, non-stop!

There's no knowing where all the extra knowledge might lead us. Maybe we'll find a limitless supply of energy without damaging our planet. Or the ability to travel at amazing speeds between the stars. Or, as incredible as it may seem, we might be able to travel through time – Einstein's theory of relativity suggests that this might be possible.

Physics knows no boundaries and the possibilities are limitless. All we need is our imagination and some scientific effort to continue this journey into the great unknown.

BE A SCIENTIST!

BE A MATHEMATI-CIAN

Amaze your friends with this maths puzzle. It works every time!

Ask a friend to think of a number and write it down. Tell them to double it. Ask them to add six. Then tell them to halve the number.

Then subtract the number they started with.

Their answer will be three!

TIP: Always ask them to add an even number, any even number, and the answer will always be half of that number. The rest is just simple maths!

MATHEMATICIAN

BE A PHYSICIST

Pick out a long iron screw, a battery, a metre of copper wire and electrical tape.

Wrap the copper wire around the screw as many times as you can, without overlapping it. Leave some wire left over on both sides of the screw.

Tape one end of the wire to one end of the battery. Attach the other side of the wire to the other end.

Guess what? You've just built your very own electro-magnet! Now you should be able to use it to pick up some light magnetic objects, like paper clips.

When you have finished experimenting, disconnect the wires. The battery will be warm, so be careful.

PHYSICIST

BE A CHEMIST

Make carbon dioxide on your tongue!

Take an orange slice and dip it in baking soda. Take a bite...

The citric acid in the orange will react with the basic baking soda, making millions of carbon dioxide bubbles.

It won't taste very nice, though!

CHEMIST

BON VOYAGE!

Thank you for coming with me on this **incredible journey**. We've come a long, long, long way together. All the way from the ginormous to the teeny-tiny, using science as our guide. I hope you've enjoyed it. I have. But then again, I'm a scientist.

HIGHWAY TO SCIENCE

We'll be scrambling to make it by Fry-day ...

But wait. So are you! We're all scientists, really. We're all interested in the world around us, using our ability to examine evidence and coming to reasonable conclusions. That's what science is.

In 1660, the world's oldest scientific organisation, the Royal Society, was founded in London. This special club was a place where scientists could meet and discuss their latest findings, or the ideas of others. It was some club, with members like Irishman Robert Boyle, Isaac Newton, Charles Darwin, Sigmund Freud, Marie Curie and Albert Einstein. And all they talked about was science.

Lots of countries followed their example and set up their own clubs. In 1785 the Royal Irish Academy was founded, which included the humanities and social sciences. (Don't worry about the word Royal – in those days you needed a king or queen to back you up, otherwise no one would listen. But anyway, aren't scientists the true royalty?!) The original Royal Society is still active today, and its motto is: **TAKE NOBODY'S WORD**.

This means that we need to find things out for ourselves. Scientists have a restless yearning for evidence. It can make us uneasy, but also hugely satisfied when we find it. And we need evidence nowadays more than ever.

We need to 'take nobody's word', because we live in an age where people come up with different conclusions for the same things; or even make up evidence altogether. You might see one fact in the news, another on the internet and hear a third in your classroom. Or read one thing about something one week, and then the opposite the next week.

Here's an example of two things you might see:

EGGS ARE KILLING YOU!

EGGS CURE ALL DISEASES!

How can you tell which is true? It's not easy, but you can try to be **MEDIA SMART** by doing three things: stop, think and check.*

First, **STOP** – especially when you've read a headline. It will catch your attention, but it can't give you the whole story. The same goes for a short social media post. Just because something has gone viral or is trending doesn't mean it's true. Things can spread fast on social media, and often for the wrong reason.

Next, **THINK**. If it sounds unbelievable, it most likely is. We all have biases, which means that we let our personal opinions influence what we think. If we come across something that agrees with them, we're more likely to believe it. I hate eggs, and I've just read eggs are bad for me. It must be true!

Finally, **CHECK**. See if the information is being reported anywhere else. If it's not, it's probably unreliable. See who is making the claims. If it's the world's biggest egg-producing company saying eggs are great, you might be more cautious. If the person who has written the piece is an influencer being paid by someone (a real Eggman), it may not be true. Is the source of the information mentioned? If there's no source, or it looks a bit off (like a bad egg) then be cautious.

Take nobody's word. Always be **SCEPTICAL**. One of Robert Boyle's most famous books was *The Sceptical Chymist* (he was hopeless at spelling, but he was a great scientist!).

*see bemediasmart.ie for more.

And what about all the things I've told you in this book? How do you know they're true? Don't only take my word for it (although I'm pretty confident what I've told you is true). **KEEP EXPLORING**. Keep finding out. The journey doesn't stop when you finish this book – you just start a new one.

You could even become a scientist yourself and discover new things. You might become a cosmologist, or a mathematician or climatologist or palaeontologist or biochemist or zoologist or immunologist or medical scientist or some type of scientist that hasn't been invented. I dare you to make a scientific discovery that nobody has ever seen before.

Sometimes, for different reasons, people have been left out of scientific history, but science is for everyone. If we only have one way of looking at the world, we're not going to be able to understand it properly. We need scientists to come from all sorts of backgrounds to continue this great **SCIENTIFIC JOURNEY**.

In this book, we began with the biggest thing in existence and finished with the smallest. You're somewhere in the middle – **ONE SINGLE PERSON** in this huge, strange, scary and fabulous universe.

This might make you feel a little insignificant. But be fearless. You're important and you can make a difference. Go on. Join the scientists.

Sure what else would you do with your precious time on this spinning lump of rock?

WE NEED YOU.

TIMELINE OF DISCOVERY

Scientists are risk takers, and they have done some crazy things. Isaac Newton stuck a needle in his eye to see what might happen. Marie Curie kept a sample of radioactive radium next to her bed as a nightlight. Barry Marshall proved that bacteria cause stomach ulcers by drinking a potion full of them. Nikola Tesla, who is famous for his work on electricity, was obsessed with the number three

and thought that he could talk to pigeons. Kevin Warwick is on a quest to become the first cyborg by implanting computer chips under his skin.* Maybe you need to be a little crazy to be a great scientist. Sometimes taking risks leads to great scientific inventions, and you'll see some of them on this page.

2,500,000 BCE | Simple stone tools are used for chopping up meat.

500,000 BCE | The first evidence of weapons appears – hunting spears

400,000 BCE | Our ancestors Homo erectus begin to use fire.

3500 BCE | The wheel is invented in Mesopotamia.

1500 BCE | The first alphabet is used by the Phoenicians.

200 BCE | The compass is used in China – but for fortune telling.

50 | Hero of Alexandria, a Greek, pioneers steam power.

105 | Chinese inventor Cai Lun makes the first paper.

808 | A formula for gunpowder appears in Chinese texts.

1000 | With his medical encyclopaedia, Al-Zahrawi becomes known as the father of surgery.

Coming through!

1021 | Physicist Ibn al-Haytham argues that light travels in straight lines.

1450 | Johannes Gutenberg introduces publishing to Europe with his printing press.

1590 | The microscope is perfected by Antonie van Leeuwenhoek.

Sorry, it seems I'm drawn to you!

1600 | Astronomer William Gilbert argues that the Earth is magnetic.

1609 | Galileo Galilei improves the telescope and discovers Jupiter's moons.

1662 | Robert Boyle proposes a law relating the volume and pressure of gases.

1687 | Isaac Newton describes the law of gravity.

1698 | Thomas Savery builds the first steam engine, which is improved by Thomas Newcomen.

1749 | American Benjamin Franklin invents the lightning conductor.

1796 | Edward Jenner popularises the smallpox vaccination.

1800 | The first battery is made by Alessandro Volta.

I might look old but I'm not a fossil.

1811 | Mary Anning begins her career as a Jurassic fossil hunter.

1821 | Michael Faraday uses an electricity generator to power a motor.

1830 | Geologist Charles Lyell argues that the Earth is millions of years old.

Hmm ... A pocket computer, you say?

1834 | Charles Babbage, helped by Ada Lovelace, designs the first computer.

1838 | Modern photography is perfected by Louis Daguerre.

1844 | Samuel Morse sends the first telegraph message.

1848 | Lord Kelvin discovers absolute zero at -273°C

1859 | Charles Darwin publishes On the Origin of Species.

1859 | The first successful internal combustion engine is created, paving the way for cars.

1876 | Alexander Graham Bell pioneers the telephone.

1895 | The movie projector is invented by the Lumière brothers in France.

1901 | Guglielmo Marconi sends radio waves across the Atlantic from Ireland.

1903 | The Wright brothers fly the first aeroplane.

1905 | Geneticists Nettie Stevens and Edmund Wilson discover sex chromosones.

It's made of precious Bakelite pearls, my lady.

1907 | The plastic age begins with the invention of Bakelite.

1909 | Ernest Rutherford's experiments reveal the structure of atoms.

1911 | Marie Curie wins a Nobel Prize for discovering polonium and radium.

1926 | Television is first demonstrated by John Logie Baird.

Surprise!

1928 | Alexander Fleming discovers penicillin by accident.

Help!

1932 | Ernest Walton and John Cockcroft split the nucleus of the atom.

1936 | Geologist Inge Lehmann realises that the Earth has a solid core.

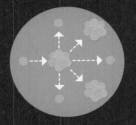

1938 | Otto Hahn, Fritz Strassmann, Lise Meitner and Otto Frisch discover and explain nuclear fission.

1942 | Enrico Fermi invents the first nuclear reactor.

1950 | British math-emetician Alan Turing devises a test for recognising artificial intelligence

1953 | DNA's structure is outlined by Francis Crick, James Watson, Maurice Wilkins and Rosalind Franklin.

Hi, partner!

1954 | The first organ transplant is performed by Dr Joseph Murray.

1957 | The space age begins when the Russians launch the first satellite, Sputnik.

1967 | Jocelyn Bell Burnell, working with Anthony Hewish, discovers a type of star called a pulsar.

1969 | The Americans rush to the moon with Apollo 11.

1977 | NASA launches its Voyager 1 and 2 probes.

Did you clean the lens, Kent? There's something dark in there ...

1978 | Astronomers Vera Rubin and Kent Ford discover evidence of dark matter in distant galaxies.

CONNECTING TO WWW WAIT 30 MIN...

1981 | The computer company IBM intro-duces its personal computer.

1989 | The World Wide Web is invented by Tim Berners-Lee.

1990 | The Hubble Space Telescope is launched.

1996 | Dolly the sheep is the first mammal to be cloned.

1997 | NASA lands its first probe on Mars.

2003 | The Human Genome Project is completed.

2004 | Facebook is launched, kicking off the age of social media.

2007 | Apple revolu-tionises mobile phones by launching the first iPhone.

2012 | Scientists find evidence of the Higgs Boson.

2016 | Oculus Rift, the first commercial virtual reality head-set, is launched.

MY PHOTO ALBUM

2019 | The first ever image of a black hole is captured.

2019 | The first commercial delivery robot is announced, called Spot.

THE FUTURE | ?

Don't try any of these things at home!

INDEX

A

absolute zero 88
aeroplane 89
ageing 59
air 30
Al-Zahrawi 88
alphabet 88
Andromeda 7
animals 26–7
Anning, Mary 88
antibiotics 58
antibodies 48
Apollo programme 15, 89
Apple iPhones 89
aquatic habitats 33
Argentinosaurus 24
asteroids 12
astronomers 7, 9, 13, 17
athletes' foot 59
atmosphere 14
atoms 66–7, 89
auroras 73
autoimmune disease 59

B

B cells 48
Babbage, Charles 88
bacteria 30, 58
Baird, John Logie 89
Bakelite 89
batteries 88
BCE (Before Common Era) 88
bees 27
Bell, Alexander Graham 89
Berners-Lee, Tim 89
Betelgeuse 11
Big Bang 6–7
biochemist 61
biologists 22, 23
Birr Castle, County Offaly 7
black hole 10, 89
blood 46
blood vessels 47
blue whale 47
Boyle, Robert 65, 86, 88
brain 42
Burnell, Dame Jocelyn Bell 11, 89
Burren, The 21

C

cacti 31, 32
Cai Lun 88
Callan, Nicholas 73
Calment, Jeanne 59
Campbell, William 59
cancer 59
carbon dioxide 30, 34
Cassini, Giovanni Domenico 13
cells 52–3
chemical energy 78
chemist 85
chemistry 64
chlorophyll 30
chromosomes 54, 89
circulatory system 46–7
climate change 34–5
climatologist 37
clones 89
Cockcroft, John 67, 89
cold-blooded animals 26
colour spectrum 81
combustion engine 88
comets 12
compass 73, 88
compounds 69
computers 71, 88, 89
constellations 11
Conway, Edward 53
cosmic ingredients 8–9
cosmic ladder 7
cosmic web 9
cosmologist 17
Crawford, Adair 69
Crick, Francis 89
Curie, Marie 89

D

Daguerre, Louis 88
dark energy 9
dark matter 9, 89
Darwin, Charles 22, 23, 88
Death Valley, California 32
deciduous trees 31
deforestation 34
Delap, Maude 33
deserts 32
digestive system 44–5
dihydrogen monoxide 69
dinosaurs 24–5
diseases 58–9

DNA 54, 55, 57, 89
Dolly the sheep 89
Doppler Effect 76
double helix 54, 55
duck-billed platypus 26

E

Earth 13, 18–19
    atmosphere 14
    continents 14
    core 89
    geology 20–1
    inner core 14
    lava 20
    magma 20
    mantle 14
    and the moon 14–15
    outer core 14
    plate tectonics 14
Einstein, Albert 82
electricity 70–1, 88
electromagnetic waves 77
electromagnetism 73, 83
electronics 70–1
elements 68–9
energy 70, 78–9
    the laws of 79
European Space Agency 13
evergreen trees 31
evolution 22–3
    human evolution 28–9
exercise physiologist 61
experiments 17, 37, 61, 85
extinction
    of dinosaurs 25
    of mammals/plants 34
extremophiles 32

F

Facebook 89
Faraday, Michael 88
FarFarOut 13
Fermi, Enrico 89
fibre-optics 81
Fitzgerald, George Francis 83
five senses 43
Fleming, Alexander 89
flowers 31
force 74–5
Ford, Kent 89
fossil fuels 34, 70

fossilised footprints 21
fossils 21, 24, 88
Franklin, Benjamin 88
Franklin, Rosalind 89
friction 74
Frisch, Otto 89
fundamental laws 82–3
fungi 30, 59

G

galaxies 7, 9, 10
galaxy clusters 9
galaxy superclusters 10
Galilei, Galileo 13, 88
genes 54–5
geneticists 55, 61
geology 20–1
geothermal energy 70
germs 48, 49, 58
Gilbert, William 88
Giotto mission 13
gravity 8, 15, 82
greenhouse gases 34
gunpowder 88
Gutenberg, Johannes 88

H

habitats 32–3
Hahn, Otto 89
Hamilton, Sir William Rowan 75
headphones 73
heart disease 59
heat energy 78
helium 68
herd immunity 49
Hero of Alexandria 88
Hewish, Anthony 89
Higgs Boson 67, 89
Himalayan jumping spider 32
homo sapiens 28, 29
Honolulu 14
Hubble Space Telescope 16, 89
human body 39, 60
    ageing 59
    brain 42
    cells 52–3
    circulatory system 46–7

digestive system 44–5
diseases 58, 59
DNA 54, 55, 57, 89
five senses 43
genes 54–5
immune system 48–9
life span 60
muscular system 41
nervous system 42
protein 56–7
reproductive system 50–1
skeleton 40
human evolution 28–9
Human Genome Project 89
Hutchins, Ellen 31
hydroelectric energy 70
hydrogen 68, 69

I

IBM computers 89
Ibn al-Haytham 88
ice ages 34
igneous rocks 20
immune system 48–9
insects 27
invertebrates 26
iPhones 89

J

Jenner, Edward 88
Joly, John 15
Jupiter 13, 88

K

Kelvin, William Thomson, 1st Baron 78, 88
kinetic energy 78

L

Laniakea supercluster 10
Large Hadron Collider 9, 67, 84
lasers 81
lava 14, 20
Lehmann, Inge 89

lenses 81
leucocytes 48
life 30
and evolution 22–3
light 80–1, 88
light waves 80
light years 6, 7
lightning conductor 88
limestone 21
lodestone 73
Longfield, Cynthia 27
Lonsdale, Dame Kathleen 69
Lovelace, Ada 88
LUCA (Last Universal Common Ancestor) 22, 23
Lumière brothers 89
Lyell, Charles 88

M

M87 (black hole) 10
McMunn, Charles 57
macrophages 48
maglev (magnetic levitation) 73
magma 20
magnetism 72–3, 88
magnetosphere 73
marble, green marble 21
Marconi, Guglielmo 89
Mars 13, 16
Mars probe 89
Mars rovers 16
Marshall, Barry 88
mass 8, 64
mathematician 85
matter 64–5
medical encyclopaedia 88
Megaw, Helen 77
Mendeleev, Dmitri 69
Mercury 12
metamorphic rocks 21
methane 34
Microraptors 25
microscope 88
Milky Way 10, 12
moon 12, 14–15
craters 15
maria (seas) 15
Moore's law 71
Morse, Samuel 88
motion 74–5
movie projector 89
MRI (magnetic resonance imager) 73
Murray, Joseph 89

muscle memory 41
muscular system 41

N

NASA 13, 15, 16, 74, 89
Neptune 13
nervous system 42
Newcomen, Thomas 88
Newton, Isaac 75, 82, 88
nuclear energy 78
nuclear fission 89
nuclear force 83
nuclear fusion 11
nuclear reactor 89

O

Oculus Rift 89
organ transplants 89
Organism 22, 27, 32
Orion Constellation 11
orthopaedist 61
oxygen 30, 69

P

palaeontologist 37
Pangaea 14
paper 88
parasites 59
Parsons, William 7
particle accelerators 67
penicillin 89
periodic table 68, 69
PH scale 65
Phoenician alphabet 88
photography 88
photons 80
photosynthesis 30
physicist 85
planets 12–13, 17
plants 30–1
plastic 89
plate tectonics 14
platypus 26
polar bears 27
polar habitats 32
pollen 31
polonium 89
potential energy 78
printing press 88
Proxima Centauri 6, 7
pulsar 11, 89
pumice 20

Q

quarks 67

R

radiation 83
radio waves 89
radium 89
rainbow 81
rainforests 33
refraction 81
renewable energy 70
reproductive system 50–1
Rigel 11
robots 89
rocket scientist 17
Royal Society, London 86
Rubin, Vera 89
Rutherford, Ernest 89

S

salt 69
Saturn 13
Savery, Thomas 88
Schrödinger, Erwin 55
science 3
and questions 86–7
timeline of discovery 88–9
sex chromosomes 89
skeleton 40
solar eclipse 15
solar energy 70
solar system 7, 12–13
space age 89
spectrum 77
speed 74
spiral galaxy 10
Sputnik 89
stars 7, 10–11
steam engine 88
steam power 88
Stegosaurus 25
Stevens, Nettie 89
stone tools 88
Strassmann, Fritz 89
sun 6, 12–13

T

T-helper cells 48
telephone 89
telescope 88
    at Birr Castle 7
    James Webb telescope 16
television 89
temperate regions 33
Tesla, Nikola 88
theory of relativity 82
timeline of discovery
    88–9
trees 31
Triceratops 24
Turing, Alan 89
Tyndall, John 81
Tyrannosaurus rex 25

U

Universe, the 4–17
    Big Bang 6–7
    cosmic ingredients
        8–9
    earth and the moon
        14–15
    the future 16
    solar system 12–13
    stars and galaxies
        10–11
Uranus 13

V

vaccination 49, 88
Valentia Island 21
van Leeuwenhoek, Antonie
    88
Venus 13
vertebrates 26
Virgo supercluster 10
virtual reality headset 89
viruses 58
volcanic islands 14
volcanoes 14
volcanologist 37
Volta, Alessandro 88
Voyager 1 13, 89

W

Wallace, Alfred Russell 23
Walton, Ernest 67, 89
warm-blooded animals 26
Warwick, Kevin 88
Watson, James 89
waves 76–7
weapons 88
Webb, James 16
wheel, invention of 88
white light 81
Wilkins, Maurice 89
Wilson, Edmund 89
WIMPS (Weakly
    Interacting Massive
    Particles) 9
wind energy 70
World Wide Web 89
Wright, Almroth 49
Wright brothers 89

Z

zero 88
zoologist 37

THANKS

LUKE

Firstly, Sarah Liddy at Gill Books who suggested I write this book and helped with content – thanks Sarah, I learnt a lot myself! To Linda Fährlin who did such gorgeous illustrations that bring the whole text alive – it's been great working with you, Linda. Thanks also to editor Sheila Armstrong who made so many great suggestions that she should really be a co-author. Many thanks Sheila – you were a joy to work with and given your scientific knowhow, I suspect you are a grandniece of Neil Armstrong. The following scientists helped with content suggestions and factchecking: Andy Gearing (frog immunologist), Humphrey Jones (biologist), Paul Nugent (physicist), Luke Drury (cosmic physicist), Mike Murphy (chemist), Sarah Corcoran (immunologist), Ciana Diskin (immunologist), Ethan Curran (future scientist), Stevie O'Neill (chemical engineer), Sam O'Neill (rocket man) and Margaret Worrall (biochemist). Thanks to all of you for helping me put together a book that will hopefully encourage our readers to join us on our great scientific adventure.

LINDA

Thank you to Sarah, Sheila and the team at Gill who made this journey from the huge to small possible. Thank you, Luke, for clarifying a lot of things, like where all the Christmas chocolates go. Thank you not only to my own teachers but all the teachers guiding the next generation of young scientists and artists. And thank you to all children for being curious! Annica and Lesley, Sligo IT. Georgia and Lou, AOI. Shells for supporting me from the beginning. Carl and Freya Brennan. Cathyanne for relaxing paddle chats about our micro universes. Martin, Ollie and Tracey at Firefly. Jessika, Henrik, Marko, Ric, Iulian at Gävle University and my course buds for the invaluable insights and laughter. My colleagues in Illustrators Ireland. Ruth, Maeve, Olga, Philip, Silv and Fred and Deirdre for all the help. The people of Sligo and my neighbours for so kindly opening your arms. Thank you to my family, Mum, Dad, Jaennice, Jacob, Rebecca and Adam for always being there. Most of all, thank you, Brian and Albin (illustrator of the cell 'heartbeat' line). I love you all the way to the moon, the stars and the never-ending universe and back.

Thanks! You're a star!

Gill Books
Hume Avenue
Park West
Dublin 12
www.gillbooks.ie

Gill Books is an imprint of M.H. Gill and Co.

Text © Luke O'Neill 2019
Illustrations © Linda Fährlin
978 07171 8558 0

Designed by www.grahamthew.com
Indexed by Eileen O'Neill

Printed by Hussar Books, Poland
This book is typeset in 11 on 14 pt Hatch regular.

The paper used in this book comes from the wood pulp of managed forests.
For every tree felled, at least one tree is planted, thereby renewing natural resources.

A CIP catalogue record for this book is available from the British Library.

10 9 8 7 6